Unwrapping the Sacred Bundle

Unwrapping
the Sacred Bundle

Reflections on the Disciplining
of Anthropology

edited by DANIEL A. SEGAL & SYLVIA J. YANAGISAKO

DUKE UNIVERSITY PRESS

Durham and London 2005

© 2005 Duke University Press

All rights reserved

Printed in the United States of America

on acid-free paper

Typeset in Charter and Melior types

by Keystone Typesetting, Inc.

Library of Congress Cataloging-in-Publication Data

appear on the last printed page of this book.

CONTENTS

Introduction

DANIEL A. SEGAL & SYLVIA J. YANAGISAKO

We start by observing a certain asymmetry. In a great many of the disciplinary contexts where we meet as anthropologists in North America, one can speak freely on behalf of "four-field anthropology," but one cannot comfortably raise questions about it. To publicly criticize the ideal of four-field anthropology—or even to acknowledge one's openness to alternatives to it—requires a willingness to be seen as "difficult." Similarly, to state that the four-field approach is not a significant component of one's anthropological work requires a willingness to have one's disciplinary credentials questioned, if not dismissed. Consider, for instance, the situation of graduate students out on the contemporary job market. Those who harbor intellectual reservations about four-field anthropology are commonly advised that it is in their best interest to refrain from expressing such views in job interviews. So too, junior faculty find that professing support for four-field anthropology functions, in some contexts, as a "loyalty oath" required for professional advancement. Is it, we ask, genuinely good for anthropology (or for anything else) that careers in our discipline so often depend upon closeting critical views of the four-field model, as if the matter were closed to reasoned and informed debate? Are such views really so dangerous? To give a different example, we have heard many colleagues, including tenured ones, tell some version of the following tale. At a meeting, of either their own department or a governance committee of the American Anthropological Association (AAA), they have found themselves listening in silent discomfort to an impassioned plea to defend "the unity" of anthropology as a "four-field" or "holistic" discipline.[1] Later, when speaking in confidence with trusted colleagues, however, they have found that other participants too had stifled their dissent so as to avoid discrediting themselves and/or disrupting the meeting's civility. Our point, in sum, is that when it comes to anthropology's "sacred bundle," divergent views do not meet on a level playing field. Rather, a particular position has been privileged, and alternatives to it are, again and again, silenced or cordoned off.[2]

This collection of papers, drawn from a panel we organized at the AAA meeting in 2000, is our attempt to foster an open debate about the definition of anthropology as a "holistic" study of humanity based on the integration of knowledge produced by the four well-known quadrants: archaeology, biological anthropology, sociocultural anthropology, and linguistic anthropology.[3] We promote such debate to explore both the effects of and alternatives to this four-field model. Because there now exists such an asymmetry in discussion about this matter in the discipline's public arena, our volume is not "balanced." Though the papers collected here are by no means in full agreement, and though some of them see more value in the four-field model than do others, we made no effort to find a contributor who would rehearse the mainstream valorization of "the four-field discipline of anthropology."[4] Such arguments can be found in any number of columns in the AAA's *Anthropology Newsletter*, many of them penned by past presidents of the AAA. So too, voices in support of this model were given a prominent place in commemorations of the AAA's centenary in 2000 and, what is more, controlled the form of those commemorations in significant ways.[5] Our purpose, by contrast, is to authorize a wider circulation of *unorthodox* voices and, in so doing, to transform an overly disciplined monologue into a transgressive dialogue—one fully open to all possible outcomes, including the refashioning, and not just the preservation, of "anthropology" as we know it now.

The title we have used for this collection—*Unwrapping the Sacred Bundle: Reflections on the Disciplining of Anthropology*—alludes to and plays off of an important paper by George Stocking, "Guardians of the Sacred Bundle: The American Anthropological Association and the Representation of Holistic Anthropology" (1988). By no stretch of the imagination does Stocking share our goal of disturbing the protected status of the four-field ideal. Nonetheless, his essay's careful historical review of "several episodes" in the history of the AAA when the unity of the four fields was "reasserted" reveals that the discipline has had centripetal tendencies at least from its Boasian onset, if not before. Moreover, by prominently reporting that some of his "colleagues at Chicago" in the 1980s spoke "disparagingly" of the four-field configuration as the "sacred bundle," Stocking—unintentionally, we are sure—gave this critical voice a wider and more public airing than did its originary speakers, who had restricted their use of the phrase to oral and informal contexts.[6] We, in turn, seek to catalyze the further circulation of this voice and to legitimate its open and unabashed use. It is in this spirit that we adopt such a voice as our own in this introduction, thereby refusing its stigma in our discipline.

Holism's Historical Consciousness

A recurring element in recent defenses of the four-field ideal is the image of an earlier "golden age" when "four-field" or "holistic" anthropology provided the discipline both intellectual unity and distinctiveness. That Boas himself had serious doubts about the coherence and stability of the four-field configuration is a point steadfastly avoided in this historical consciousness (Stocking 1960, 1988; see also Yanagisako this volume and Clifford this volume). Instead, in affirmations of the four-field model, the discipline's past (and most particularly, its Boasian past) is rendered free of such complexity, thereby producing a baseline for an apocalyptic narrative of the discipline's descent from earlier "unity" to present-day "Balkanization." Serving as a moral tale that warns of the demise of the discipline if such fragmentation is not reversed, this narrative presents us with the binary choice of defending the four-field model or losing anthropology altogether—as if "anthropology" was not a contingent formation but a fixed entity defined by a transhistoric essence instantiated in the four-field "sacred bundle."

The rhetorical figure of the discipline's endangerment by contemporary fragmentation—with the suggestion that if we do not preserve anthropology, we betray it—can be found in myriad contexts. A case in point is the debate over the reorganization of the AAA that took place at the end of the 1990s. In January 1997, a Commission to Review the Organizational Structure of the AAA was appointed by the AAA Executive Committee and charged to suggest a reorganization plan that would "capture and sustain the *unity* of our discipline" (Moses 1997; emphasis added).[7] In a report that gave its highest priority to strengthening the four-field configuration of the discipline, the commission quoted, in turn, the dire assessment of the AAA's "Long Range Plan": "at the moment when the need and potential for anthropological knowledge to address human problems has never been greater, the discipline in the U.S. is fragmented, in many cases too self-absorbed, and, some would argue, in danger of splintering into extinction, or, at best, becoming a marginal observer" (Commission to Review the Organizational Structure 1997, 8). The commission's concomitant call to salvage the "unity" of the discipline had the familiar ring of revitalization rhetoric, all the while depending upon selective amnesia about, if not an active misremembering of, what was in actuality a plural and contested past.

Accommodations to Four-Field Holism

The privileging of the four-field model and the stifling of open inquiry into it can be found as well in various organizational and pedagogic schemes adopted by departments of anthropology at U.S. colleges and universities. At particular moments in the recent past, a small number of departments—Emory's being the most prominent—have committed themselves wholeheartedly to the pursuit of "holism," in both teaching and research activities.[8] Though we are skeptical about the fruitfulness of such endeavors, we recognize and give credit to them as principled and coherent intellectual programs. Many more departments, however, combine explicit affirmations of the four-field ideal—on their websites, in course catalogs, and in documents prepared for various kinds of institutional reviews, for instance—with a collegial compartmentalization of the discipline's different wings, allowing each quadrant substantial autonomy over such matters as hiring, promotions, and, with the exceptions we discuss below, curricular offerings. Faculty housed in such confederated arrangements will often acknowledge, if only sotto voce, that their department is primarily an administrative umbrella and that the "cohabitation" of the four fields does little to promote dialogue between cultural anthropologists interested in, say, transnational migration and biological anthropologists interested in, say, human osteology.

In such cases, whatever the relative strength of the quadrants, intellectual discord among them is treated like a "family secret." In particular, departments often maintain the fiction of four-field unity in their dealings with administrators. This reticence reflects the received wisdom that "holism," however little it is practiced, is an effective way of representing anthropology in the pursuit of resources and public authority. One wonders, though, whether such an approach—"strategic holism," let us call it—is in the end the most effective means to obtain support for diverse anthropologies. Does marketing anthropology as a "biocultural synthesis" really increase the material support for, or the authority of, say, studies of the myriad ways particular regimes of power and domination are naturalized? We think not. Rather, in our view, such work would be better served by making the strongest case possible, in the academy and beyond, for the importance of the distinctive analytic strengths of cultural-social anthropology as it is widely practiced today—that is, as an interpretive social science grounded, at once, in fine-grained ethnographic reporting and the foregrounding of contingency by means of wide-ranging comparison across cultures.[9]

Undergraduates at U.S. colleges and universities are a second audience that, more often than not, is shielded from anthropology's "family secret" of intradisciplinary discord. At many schools, anthropology departments offer undergraduates a four-field introductory course, both as a point of entry into the major and as a broad sample of the discipline for students who go on to pursue other majors. As a rule, students in such courses are told that the discipline of anthropology is defined by a "holistic" integration of the studies of human biology, linguistics, cultures, and prehistory—even though such a "holistic" approach is effectively absent from both upper-level courses in the very same department and the scholarly work of most (if not all) departmental faculty. Many single-quadrant introductory courses similarly begin by defining anthropology in terms of "holism" and "biocultural integration," as is evidenced by most of the textbooks available for the teaching of sociocultural introductory courses.[10] In either case, starting with the four-field model—or more precisely, situating that model as a starting point for further study in anthropology—presents four-field "holism" as a "foundation" that supports and encompasses the more "specialized" quadrants of the discipline. This, in effect, preempts the alternative view—that is, that the four-field model is nothing less and nothing more than a distinct paradigmatic tradition within the contested terrain we speak about as "anthropology."

Given these consequences, it is important to consider why colleagues with reservations about the four-field model do so little to resist this pedagogic sequencing. It is all too clear, for instance, that the reward structure for faculty, particularly at our most prestigious research universities, makes it attractive for scholars with dissenting views to accept the status quo rather than to invest time in remaking (and thereafter teaching) their department's introductory-level course or courses. So too, one can see that faculty with the greatest commitment to "four-field holism" would be drawn, more so than other faculty, to teaching at the introductory level, since they are likely to perceive that more advanced courses do not afford them the "breadth" needed to teach the four-field model.[11]

In addition, this common pedagogic sequencing, in which four-field holism comes first and alternatives to it come later, is commonly propped up by the argument that it is best for students to learn the more orthodox (or "mainstream") view of the discipline before being exposed to "the critiques." Let us note, however, that this defense presumes its own conclusion, since it takes for granted—rather than makes an argument for—the claim that "holism" should be accorded its current "mainstream" status in the discipline. Worse yet, this defense overlooks the fact that many, if not most, students who take an introductory course in anthropology will never take an additional course in the discipline and will thus never be exposed to the "critiques" deferred. In sum, the sequencing of different anthropologies in the undergraduate curriculum is neither even-handed nor neutral. Rather, it "protects" students from some of the most innovative and provocative perspectives in the discipline, including critiques of culturally dominant orthodoxies.[12]

It is further worth noting that at many universities, the foundational status of "the four fields" is reinscribed in requirements that doctoral students, regardless of their quadrant or area of specialization, obtain some training in each of the four fields. Such requirements gain support even from many faculty who are skeptical about their intellectual merits on the grounds that they prepare graduate students to teach a four-field introductory course at the undergraduate level and thereby make them more employable. The pedagogic accommodation to four-field holism at the undergraduate level thus has a direct and congruent effect at the graduate level. In addition, many graduate students participate in undergraduate courses outside their own quadrant as teaching assistants. In such cases, they encounter the knowledge of another quadrant or quadrants in a context in which there is little opportunity for independent thinking and critical engagement: teaching assistants are not, after all, paid to interrogate a course professor's lectures.[13] This too means that in graduate training, as in undergraduate programs, students are likely to be socialized into some minimal, yet sturdy, acceptance of the orthodox status of the four-field model and its constituent quadrants.

Finally, it is worth observing one of the ways that the privileging of the four-field model has played out in recent years in the activities of the AAA. In this context, the *American Anthropologist* (*AA*), which is published by the AAA, has been increasingly freighted with the obligation to represent disciplinary "unity." In most general terms, this has occurred in response to the growing epistemological divergence of different forms of anthropology, notably between biological and cultural approaches within the discipline. More concretely, this has occurred in response to two prominent material manifestations of this intellectual divergence—the first being the emergence and rise to prominence of subfield journals produced by various sections of the AAA (starting with the publication of the *American Ethnologist* by the American Ethnological Society in 1974) and the second being the decision of most biological anthropologists to leave the AAA in the context of the association's reorganization in the early 1980s.[14] Taken together, these episodes and the intellectual tensions that shaped them have given *AA* an intensified, and in many ways quite novel, responsibility to stand for disciplinary "unity." This, in turn, has resulted in various barriers to publication in *AA* of work perceived by four-field advocates to be a betrayal of that "unity." One thinks here of work that takes strongly constructivist positions or work that argues for the fictiveness of anthropological knowledge. The barriers to such work have, in some instances, taken the form of public attacks, vicious at times, aimed at *AA* editors deemed insufficiently loyal to the four-field model.[15] We (as bystanders, not participants) have also observed such barriers in the editorial direction given to authors, as when authors have been instructed to drop sections of articles that treat the discipline's "scientific" status as contested, whether in the past or present. Ironically, however, the requirement that *AA* serve as the icon of four-field "unity" has meant that in recent decades, precious little cutting-edge work in cultural-social anthropology has appeared in the journal. To give an example that illustrates this point, in 1974, the year when the single quadrant *American Ethnologist* first appeared, we find published in *AA*, James Boon and David Schneider's "Kinship vis-à-vis Myth: Contrasts in Levi-Strauss' Approaches to Cross-Cultural Comparison." Over the subsequent three decades, we would suggest, it has become more difficult for a piece so unabashedly antipositivist to be published in the AAA's "flagship" journal.[16]

The Social-Evolutionary Burden of Holism

As cultural-social anthropologists, we find ourselves skeptical about the four-field model for a number of related reasons. To begin with, we note that four-field anthropology has never meant just an abstract "holism"; it has always involved something more concrete than this term indicates on its own. At the substantive level of the purview of anthropological inquiry, for instance, it has meant a bundling together of three primary topics: non-European peoples (their "societies," "cultures," and "languages"); human relics (both material artifacts and skeletal remains); and non-human primates (both monkey and ape). These three areas of inquiry cohered—or rather were sutured—as "anthropology" in the wake of the revolution in human time of the mid-nineteenth century, in which the short biblical chronology of human existence was displaced by the long secular chronology. In the context of this new comprehension of human time, what brought together these research areas was the notion that all three offered evidence of what human life had been in the distant recesses of the human past, all the way back to the (much mythologized) moment of human origin.[17] It thus can be said that anthropology's much vaunted "holism" was, at its initial crystallization, motivated by the identification of darker-skinned persons with the segment of time/development located as *pre-* to both "history" and "civilization." Thus, whatever else anthropological holism has been—and we allow that it has been more than just this—it has been a carrier of the social-evolutionary figure of the division of humanity into a civilizational Self and relatively backward (less and pre-civilized) Others.

That this social-evolutionary figure was objectified and institutionalized as "four-field anthropology" in the North American context, but not on the other side of the Atlantic, is no accident (see also Yanagisako this volume). It is crucial to these different outcomes that in the Americas, all that was *pre-* to "history" (which, in the American context, is conventionally construed to be everything *pre-* to Columbus) was registered as being discontinuous with "whites" and "Europeans"; anything and everything from the long ago was "native," as in the identity term *Native American.* This included not only material artifacts from earlier chronological moments, but also the "disappearing" languages and cultures, and the very bodies, of living Native Americans. In continental Europe and Britain, by contrast, the most accessible "remnants" of the time before "history" were—or to be more precise, *were registered as*—"European." So too, these "remnants" were designated as belonging to the past of a particular nationality within the overarching European identity category. As a result— that is, because both the broad European identity and its component national identities were extended back into the time before history (and specifically into the Neolithic era)—the study of *pre*-ness was fissured. Folklore, peasant studies, and Neolithic archaeology emerged in close association with disciplinary history, sociology, and classics, as so many ways of studying Europe and its national kinds; concomitantly, these fields were set apart from social anthropology (meaning ethnographic studies of living non-Europeans) and the study of hominid evolution (see also Hodder this volume). Thus in the British and continental European contexts, the decomposition of humanity into "European" and "non-European" disrupted the institutionalization of holism, while this very same decomposition of humanity supported this institutionalization on the other side of the Atlantic. The difference was that in the so-called Old World, "European" identity was extended back before history, whereas in America, there was a coincidence of the division of time and racialized identity distinctions.

For our purposes, the important question is not which of these disciplinary arrangements was better or worse in its day (that question is moot in any case). Rather, the question with which we—a pronoun that should be read as referring to anthropologists in general and to anthropologists located in the North American "four-field" context in particular—must grapple now is whether it is possible to continue to produce four-field journals, textbooks, introductory courses, departments, and so on and *not* recirculate the social-evolutionary allegory of the *pre*-ness of non-European Others.

We (in this instance, the editors of this volume) are aware that some who are attached to the four-field model hope to overcome the social-evolutionary baggage of "holism" by broadening the empirical horizons of sociocultural and linguistic anthropologies so that these subfields no longer gaze primarily or disproportionately on non-European peoples. The study of hominid evolution, apes, and various old stuff would, as a consequence, be linked to the study of "humanity" overall, rather than to the study of non-European Others—and anthropological "holism" would, mercifully, escape its social-evolutionary past.

Yet as much as we are drawn in principle to this project of a radical redistribution of the ethnographic gaze, we think it is naive to imagine that anthropology can so easily control either its own composition or its own signification. What is overlooked in imagining this future for four-field anthropology is that no matter how fully anthropology itself disowns "the savage slot" (Trouillot 1991), it will not be freed of its association with non-European Others *as long as other disciplines in the human sciences, such as history and sociology, retain their disproportionate focus on "the West" and/or "Western" subjects.* In short, anthropology's attachment to "the savage slot" is not located solely in the discipline's own activities; rather, that attachment is lodged at least as much in a larger system of disciplinary distinctions—over which anthropology has only a limited say. Indeed, we would note that in the larger multidisciplinary context of the academy, when anthropologists increase the attention they devote in their research and teaching to Europe and its diaspora, the unintended result, in most cases, is a proportionate decline in such attention, overall in the academy, to the study of such places as Africa and Oceania. In short, unless other humanities and social science disciplines become more robustly globalized, the "repatriation" of anthropology unwittingly risks contributing to the academy's provincialism. The more general lesson here is that in analyzing anthropology's relationship to Otherness, we must shift from thinking about "anthropology" in isolation to locating anthropology in its interdisciplinary and institutional relationships.

In this spirit, let us observe that the very fact that "holism" has remained within anthropology and has not spread to such disciplines as history and sociology suggests that it continues to bear a social-evolutionary burden. Had some more theoretically legitimate basis for the integrated four-field study of human phenomena emerged over the course of the twentieth century, such holism would long since have left anthropology per se and been embraced by these discipline of the Western Self. Indeed, it is striking that so few advocates of four-field anthropology have urged their colleagues in these disciplines to adopt this same model—holding, for instance, that scholars of the French Revolution, as much as scholars of Balinese cockfights, need to control knowledge of the posture of Australopithecus and the polymorphous sex lives of Bonobo apes. One can, then, at least credit evolutionary psychologists and sociobiologists with a principled even-handedness, since they hold, and with much certainty too, that their forms of biological determinism apply to the West as much as the rest. Yet, though sociobiology and evolutionary psychology have had moments of ascendancy in scholarly debate, they have to date not been taken seriously as a basis for remaking, say, history as a "holistic" discipline. In sum, the perduring linkage of holism to anthropology—and not to the human sciences more generally—reveals a persistence of a social-evolutionary scheme in which non-European peoples are identified with *pre-* ness.

Your Response, Please

We thus are brought to ask the following question of our colleagues in cultural-social anthropology who argue for holding on to holism: when was the last time that research on hominid evolution or primates was helpful to you in thinking about your ethnographic data? To date, we have seen little evidence that so-called biocultural syntheses offer cultural-social anthropology (or linguistic anthropology) a useful tool. To the contrary, rather than contributing to interesting work in cultural-social anthropology, such syntheses seem most often to have been designed to control and limit cultural-social anthropology, making it less rather than more interesting in at least two ways. First, though presented as *syntheses*, these approaches offer instead acts of *reduction*—specifically, the reduction of the cultural and social to the biological. In this sense, such supposed syntheses operate to reinforce the Comtean model, in which cultural and social phenomena are reducible to biology, which, in turn, is reducible to the laws governing inanimate matter (as studied by chemistry and physics), which, finally, are reducible to mathematics. This overlooks and obscures the ways human agents project cultural schemes into the material world, creating hybrid empirical phenomena—peoples and genders, to give just two examples—that are never reducible to a pre-cultural nature or reality, even if they cannot violate that reality.[18] Second (and this point echoes one we made previously in discussing the history of the *American Anthropologist* in recent decades), calls for four-field holism and biocultural integration are often, in our experience, thinly disguised attacks on those strands of cultural-social anthropology—specifically interpretive and constructivist approaches—most visibly in tension with positivism (see, for example, the discussion of the relationship of anthropology to "science" published in the *Anthropology Newsletters* of March, April, May, and October 1996).[19]

It is no coincidence, then, that heightened appeals for a "return" to four-field "unity" have accompanied the increasing engagement of cultural-social anthropologists, linguistic anthropologists, and postprocessual archaeologists in productive dialogue with scholars in the humanities. These appeals often go hand in hand with attempts to erect boundaries between anthropology and the humanities, insisting—without offering evidence—that there are more productive conversations to be had with the natural sciences. The fear that too active a dialogue with the humanities will result in the downgrading of anthropology from a social science to a humanities discipline has incited the now familiar humanities-bashing, which so often takes the form of lumping any and all nonpositivist approaches to cultures and societies into the demonized category of "postmodernism." Once again, a selective memory of the discipline's history, in which dialogue with the humanities has been integral to the contributions of theorists from Morgan to Boas and from Sapir to Geertz, fuels the argument for shunning the "soft" pleasures of humanistic approaches for the presumed payoff of closer association with positivist approaches to culture and society. These appeals assume a zero-sum game in which dialogue with the humanities precludes dialogue among the four fields and between anthropology and the natural sciences; likewise, they do not bother to spell out how a revitalization of dialogue among the four fields will lead to productive research agendas and theory development.

Our point is not, however, to suggest that it is never useful to bring cultural and biological knowledges into cooperative dialogue. Clearly it has been and continues to be fruitful and strategic to bring both of these forms of knowledge to bear on racial theories of human difference. Yet in our view, the project of contesting racial thinking is best served not by appealing to the authority of a singular "anthropological science" but by highlighting the *different* strengths of biological and cultural analyses of "race." Population biology, for instance, is crucial for demonstrating that, by the very criteria that allow us to see objective distinctions among biological species, there is no basis for holding that there are distinct races of *homo sapiens*. By contrast, it is cultural analysis that allows us to understand the various and contingent ways that fictive races have been projected into the material world and mistaken for objective facts from roughly the seventeenth century up to and through the present.

Furthermore, though we fully embrace such complementary (rather than integrated or synthesized) uses of cultural and biological knowledges, what we see as most valuable in anthropology's four-field past is something even more at variance with the ideal of the "unity" of anthropological knowledge. It is something that is nicely suggested by recalling that Boas's contributions to the "physical" quadrant of his day were primarily *negative*. In other words, Boas's work in physical anthropology served primarily to implode, rather than to extend or develop, an active line of inquiry in physical anthropology—specifically, research into racial character and differences.[20] This negative but immensely important achievement was the result of neither "holism" nor "biocultural integration"; nor, moreover, was it a consequence of adhering to some singular "scientific method," as those who today claim a monopoly on "scientific" anthropology would lead us to expect.[21] Rather, Boas's success in critiquing racial anthropology was the product of a complex cluster of intellectual dispositions that, taken together, laid the foundation for the Boasian tradition. These dispositions included: (i) a propensity to be suspicious in the face of the convergence of scientific claims, on the one hand, and both social prejudice and ethnocentrism, on the other; (ii) a critical empiricism that sought to grapple with, rather than to deny, the difficulties raised by the recognition that human observation is always already socialized; and (iii) an epistemological stance that holds that there are no insignificant human "cases," meaning that knowledge of "humanity" must be based as much on the exotic as on the familiar.

To put this in somewhat different terms, advocates of four-field "holism" characteristically (and persistently) seek for anthropology the status of a "normal science," to borrow Kuhn's (1996 [1962]) phrase. Rather than valuing the destabilizing possibility of critical dialogue across different forms of knowledge, they pursue the *integration* of diverse anthropologies into a singular, dominant paradigm. They thus seek to close down the very problematizing of knowledge that cultural-social anthropology and its relativizing so often produce. We, by contrast, embrace the very dispositions that have made cultural-social anthropology both an unsettled and an unsettling science. This is to say, we embrace cultural-social anthropology as a "queer science," rather than a "normal" one— that is, as a science whose greatest achievements have been to sustain and deepen struggles against a range of mainstream and dominant ideas about humanity, including racial formalism, social evolutionism, bourgeois economism, and naturalized gender hierarchies, among others.[22]

As we have already signaled, this volume is unabashedly interested. The essays we have included share a common goal of opening up rather than shutting down discussion about our discipline's configuration. Yet, though none of the contributions in this volume participate in the project of promoting four-field orthodoxy, they do not otherwise converge on a single position or stance.

Jim Clifford's essay takes up a position that is largely, though not fully, on the outside of anthropology "looking in." Clifford examines the "academic disciplining processes" that have defined the anthropological niche within a larger field of possibilities. Using comparison and a wide-angled field of vision, he shows us that disciplinary contingency is less a distinctive "problem" of anthropology than an underlying condition of all disciplines, even those that today appear most "necessary." Clifford's primary example in this regard is "history." Any university lacking a department of history, he observes, would be discredited as incomplete, something that is not true for a university lacking a department of anthropology by contrast. Yet, argues Clifford, it is possible to imagine an intellectually vibrant university where "history" as a department does not exist, assuming that historical knowledge and thinking were dispersed into and throughout other disciplines, including the natural sciences. For Clifford, a key lesson of this thought experiment is that disciplinary disestablishment need not be regarded as pathological.

A second important issue Clifford addresses is why anthropology today seems more fragmented than it had seemed for much of the twentieth century. On Clifford's account, the earlier sense of disciplinary coherence was based on the "articulation" of "(1) an empirical object, (2) a distinctive method, (3) an interpretive paradigm, and (4) a telos or transcendent object." As Clifford explains this "articulation": "The object was 'primitive' societies; the method was 'fieldwork'; the paradigm was 'culture'; the telos was 'Man.'" In recent decades, however, each of these elements has been subjected to intense critique, thereby making each of them on its own, and consequently their "articulation," a less settled and self-evident matter.

To this argument, we would add the following observation: the earlier assumption that the empirical study of seemingly primitive societies was a privileged means of studying "human nature" took support from two quite distinct propositions, both of which we have already mentioned in this introductory essay. One of these was the social-evolutionary idea that non-European Others offered evidence of human origins and, by implication, humanity's essential and unvarnished nature; the second of these was the Boasian view that there are no insignificant human cases, however "primitive," small-scale, or otherwise Other. The first of these propositions is one we abhor; the second is one we see as vital for any valid science of societies, cultures, and histories. We thus are led to the painful irony that the disciplinary bundle that Clifford describes as having been accepted in the earlier period of disciplinary "normalcy" (again in the Kuhnian sense) was supported by both egregious and admirable elements of the discipline's complex past.

Rena Lederman's essay focuses on anthropology's relationship to the nonacademic public sphere and draws conclusions that diverge in significant ways from Clifford's. Using the recent controversy over Chagnon's work with the Yanomani as an illustrative case, Lederman argues that whether we like it or not, the media represent our disciplinary knowledge as being about "humanity" and its fundamental "nature." To disengage from the discussion of this four-field "telos" (to return to Clifford's vocabulary) is thus to abdicate responsibility for public education. Moreover, if anthropology or certain strands of the discipline were to refuse to address these larger questions, media inquiries about "human nature" would nonetheless be answered by those who are not deterred by a recognition of its fictiveness: sociobiologists, evolutionary psychologists, rational choice theorists, and so on. At a certain level of abstraction, then, Lederman's essay converges with our observation above that anthropology does not control its own fate, though whereas we observed constraints within the academy, Lederman finds them outside.

Lederman also seeks to remind us of the fruitfulness of various ad hoc formations—reading groups, edited volumes, and so on—assembled from four-field ingredients at particular moments in the past in relation to specific questions or research agendas. Recalling the value of these non-formulaic and problem-focused uses of four-field resources, Lederman argues that we should continue to draw strategically, if contingently, on the four-field tradition, even as we contest its orthodoxy. For Lederman then, more than for any other contributor in this volume, the four-field model continues to be salient, both in more broadly public contexts and within the field of anthropological inquiry itself.

Sylvia Yanagisako's essay offers a more critical view of the four-field tradition. Emphasizing the North American context of the four-field project (and supplementing the argument presented above), Yanagisako argues that holism's linkage of social-evolutionary and cultural approaches is grounded in, and continues to reinscribe, "ideological processes of settler colonialism." More specifically, she finds in anthropological "holism" the traces of an earlier project of acquiring knowledge about Native Americans in the service of forging a distinctive national identity for the continent's post-Columbian whites and their settler-centered, Indian-dominating nation-states. From Lewis Henry Morgan's "pioneering" ethnological study of the Iroquois in the mid-nineteenth century to the ethical-retributive attempts to "salvage" Native American culture in the early twentieth century, the "Americanist" tradition of anthropology has been saturated with sentiments of settler-colonial nationalism. Contemporary cultural anthropology, Yanagisako argues, should neither honor nor uphold this legacy and its "uneasy alliance" of "evolutionary adaptationist" and "cultural" perspectives. It should instead pursue flexible arrangements for knowledge production and transmission, arrangements that are as fully open to dialogues with other disciplines as they are to dialogues with other quadrants of anthropology. Thus, in contrast to Lederman's position, the "flexible disciplinarity" Yanagisako advocates does not keep one hand grasped around the sacred bundle, even contingently.

Given the divergences between their essays, it is worth noting that Lederman and Yanagisako both contextualize their own intellectual position at least in part in terms of the department that has employed them in their respective careers. Thus Lederman observes that as a faculty member in a purely sociocultural department, she has been shielded from the intradisciplinary conflicts that have plagued many four-field departments in recent decades; Yanagisako, by contrast, points at "the conflict that led to the division of Stanford's Department of Anthropology" to support her claim that the intellectual tensions within "the sacred bundle" are often far from productive.

Michael Silverstein's contribution to this volume is distinctive in focusing on the history and effects of convergence, rather than divergence, between subfields. He is concerned in particular with parallel theoretical developments in linguistic and cultural anthropologies—two subfields that between the world wars seemed significantly at odds, as George

Stocking (1992a, 152–155) has reminded us. When all is said and done, Silverstein's complex and nuanced argument suggests that the convergence in these subfields has, ironically, contributed to the unmaking and disarticulation of the four-field model.

Silverstein locates the convergence between linguistic and cultural anthropologies in their shared recognition that their presumed subjects of inquiry—"languages" and "cultures"—are something other than discrete, bounded, and countable objects. Over many decades, Silverstein argues, both subfields have slowly come to understand that the observable boundaries between two "languages" or between two "cultures" are made rather than simply found. It follows that it is a fallacy to treat rosters of so many "languages" or so many "cultures" as sets of independent and comparable "cases" that can be examined so as to discover "scientific laws" pertaining to each roster, be it "human languages" or "human cultures." The items placed into these rosters are not comparable cases because their delineations are inescapably historical and contingent, reflecting local circumstances and diverse social projects, rather than following some invariant analytic criterion (such as mutual unintelligibility). In a nontrivial sense, then, "English," "Swahili," and "Indonesian" are not so much three cases or instances of a common type (three "languages") as they are three disparate scoops of human stuff that have each been constructed as, and thus given the status of, "a language."

Read most radically, Silverstein's argument allows us to imagine the collapse of the very distinction between linguistic and cultural phenomena. If there is nothing necessary or objective about the delineation of a certain bundle of conventionalized practices of communication as a "language," then it follows that the particular phonemic, semantic, and syntactical phenomena in that delineated bundle do not possess or exhibit a *necessary* unity (though such an integration may well be imposed on and given to them) *qua* "a language." But this, in turn, implies that the identification of this trio of phenomena as *linguistic,* as distinct from other phenomena that we identify as *cultural* (habits of body movements, practices of material circulation, and so on), is itself a contingent practice of anthropology and the social sciences more broadly. In the end, then, Silverstein's argument leaves us with a more open field of linguistic-cultural processes and gradient differences—a field whose very decomposition into linguistic phenomena, on the one hand, and cultural phenomena, on the other, is contingent and historical rather than natural and fixed. Recall the very title of Silverstein's essay: "Languages/Cultures Are Dead! Long Live the Linguistic-Cultural!"

Though Silverstein's essay does not explicitly address questions of institutional organization and politics, his deconstruction of the language/cultural binary raises question about the practice of treating "linguistic anthropology" and "cultural anthropology" as distinct quadrants—as, for instance, in the organization of the AAA and in college and university departments. So too, though in his case explicitly, Ian Hodder's essay opens up the question of whether "anthropology" provides the best institutional home for archaeology—or better, various archaeologies. Hodder's concerns echo Yanagisako's, for Hodder sees archaeology's residence in four-field anthropology as constraining archaeologists' potentially fruitful avenues of exploration with both the natural sciences and the humanities. Moreover, just as Clifford guides us in imagining historical knowledge and thinking liberated from the confines of a singular disciplinary house, Hodder suggests that a range of different and interesting archaeologies might emerge were archaeology to be dispersed and thereafter linked, in different ways, with classics, history, human biology, cultural-social anthropology, environmental science, and so on. Postprocessual archaeology, which Hodder has been a leader in forging, has drawn both from interpretive approaches in cultural-social anthropology and from the reflexive turn in the social sciences and humanities, for example. Moreover, Hodder's personal experience of forging strategic alliances that cut across disciplines and fields—including his transatlantic move from an archaeology department to a department of cultural and social anthropology—is an apt illustration of both Clifford's model of disciplines as contingent articulations and Yanagisako's figure of flexible disciplinarity.

A thematic convergence among the contributions in this volume—even as they differ in the implications and prescriptions they draw from it—is an interactionist model of disciplinary formation and transformation. Rather than defining anthropology as an essential core—whether of distinctive theories, methods, or questions—all the contributors treat anthropology as forged through encounters, exchanges, and articulations within and beyond academia. In this sense, they all position themselves against a patriotic disciplinarity that calls for internal unity and a defense of borders against foreign threat.

As editors of this volume, we are keenly aware that anthropology is too protean and rich to be refashioned along the lines of any "master plan," and neither we nor this volume offers one. Rather, our hope is that this collection of essays will remap the lines of acceptable debate, opening up productive and reasoned discussion of the four-field model and alternatives to it.

NOTES

Thanks to Richard Handler, Laurie Shrage, Claudia Strauss, and Duke University Press's anonymous reviewers for careful readings of earlier drafts of this introductory essay. Thanks also to Adria LaVioletta for advice on editorial matters regarding this collection of papers.

1. Here and elsewhere in the essay, we hold that the terms *four-field* and *holistic*, while not strictly synonyms, are frequently and facilely used in place of each other, and for very much the same purposes, in characterizing and providing a defining label for "anthropology." In this regard, these terms require some additional comment. We recognize that *holistic* is used in two distinct, though to our observation rhetorically linked, senses in representations of "anthropology." This is nicely evidenced by the textbooks used to teach introductory-level courses at colleges and universities in the United States. To give a quite typical example, Nanda and Warms's *Cultural Anthropology* first tells readers that "to say anthropology is *holistic* means that it combines the study of human biology, history, and the learned and shared patterns of behavior and thought we call culture" (2002, 2; emphasis in original); this text then proceeds immediately to introduce the discipline's major subfields, effectively identifying the composite of these subfields with anthropology's "holistic" character. However, once the text has shifted from its prefatory discussion of *anthropology* as an overall field of study to an overview of *cultural anthropology* (the subject designated as the text's focus by its title), it introduces a second sense of *holistic*, defining it in terms of the integrated study of the "subsystems" of *culture*—that is, an analysis that brings together, say, religion, economics, politics, family life, and so on (81). Interestingly, the glossary entry for the term *holism* in this same textbook sutures the two senses of the term (422). In relation to our introductory essay and volume, it is sufficient to note that our concern is with the first of these notions of *holistic* rather than the second. Nonetheless, it is also worth observing that the presence in this (and other) textbooks of two versions of *holistic*—one pertaining to the study of humanity and the other to the study of culture—indexes the stature and authority this term has in representations of the discipline.

This same textbook also illustrates an important point about the designation of anthropology as a "four-field discipline." When this text lists and names the discipline's primary subfields, it includes "applied anthropology" as a fifth subfield, along with the standard four (here named as "cultural anthropology," "linguistic anthropology," "archaeology," and "physical or biological anthropology"). Nonetheless, even though the identification of an additional subfield or subfields is not idiosyncratic to this textbook, the phrase *four-field discipline* remains entrenched as a standard label—a nickname almost—for the discipline. In a nontrivial sense, then, the term *four-field discipline* does not simply, or even primarily, serve to specify a particular number of subfields; rather, it is often used to index and affirm the *reach* of anthropology, from *biology* to *culture*, and as such, the discipline's supposedly *holistic* character.

2. Here and subsequently in this introductory essay, our comments draw at times on our experiences as participants in the governance structure of the AAA. Given that these experiences provide ethnographic grounding for many of the arguments presented here, it seems appropriate to note the primary capacities in which we have participated in AAA governance. Sylvia Yanagisako served on the AAA Executive Committee in 1998–1999; Daniel Segal is at this time serving on that committee and is also the convener of the AAA's Section Assembly. Yanagisako served on the editorial board of the *American Anthropologist* (AA) (the AAA's only "four-field" journal) during Robert Sussman's terms as editor; Segal has served on that board during the term of AA's current editors, Francis Mascia-Lees and Susan Lees. Both served two-year terms as president of the Society for Cultural Anthropology, a "section" of the AAA. Finally, Segal served a five-year term (1998–2002) on the Nominations Committee of the AAA.

3. There is, of course, some variation in the labels used for each quadrant. Some of this variation has resulted from attempts to mark and herald the emergence of a new approach or school of thought within a quadrant, as with the shift from "physical" to "biological" anthropology.

4. Our intent here is to quote the voice of convention within the discipline; the particular wording we use here to exemplify that voice is taken from a section title from yet another standard introductory-level textbook, Hicks and Gwynne's *Cultural Anthropology* (1996, 3).

5. For example, the AAA Centennial Commission commemorated the AAA's achievements in scientific publishing by producing a volume of selected papers that had been published in *AA* in the years subsequent to the previous moment of associational commemoration, some twenty-five years earlier. At the time of the seventy-fifth anniversary of the founding of the AAA, the association had produced three volumes of this sort, each of which covered roughly a quarter-century of the AAA's existence to that point. There was, however, significant incommensurability between this form of commemoration at the seventy-fifth and centenary junctures. The period covered by the centenary volume (1971–1995) differed from the earlier periods in that before 1974, the *AA* was the AAA's only journal. From 1974 on, by contrast, various sections of the AAA began sponsoring new journals, such as *American Ethnologist* and the *Journal of Linguistic Anthropology*. Thus in the later period, the AAA's scientific publishing did not reside solely in the *AA* but was dispersed among many journals. Moreover, for some of the years in this new era of AAA journal publishing, the citation rates for articles in journals other than *AA* surpassed those for articles in *AA*. Nonetheless, the AAA Centennial Commission

rejected a proposal to frame its commemorative volume as selected papers from AAA's journals rather than selected papers from the AA, with this decision justified in terms of the importance of affirming the "unity" of anthropology as a "four-field discipline."

6. There seems to be no record of who coined the phrase, and our informal efforts to track down such an originating source in 2002—involving phone calls and e-mails to Stocking, who in turn consulted colleagues from the earlier moment—yielded only a list of "the usual suspects" as possibilities.

7. "Are Four Fields in Our Future?" AAA president Yolanda Moses's preamble to the text of the report by the Commission to Review the Organizational Structure of the AAA.

8. For a sense of the Emory project, see Paul 1987. This was a special issue of the journal *Cultural Anthropology*, comprised only of articles by Emory anthropologists, for the purpose of showcasing the department's distinctive project and character.

9. We have noted that scholars working in the discipline's quadrants have at various moments introduced and attempted to establish new labels for a given quadrant to indicate a historical shift in its character or form. Here we ourselves operate in this vein, deploying the less standard term *cultural-social*, rather than *sociocultural*, anthropology. In adopting this term, we wish to mark the emergence, since the mid-twentieth century, of a more explicitly theoretical practice in this quadrant and with it a renewed foregrounding of contingency or culturalness, though conceived adjectivally rather than nominally, that is, conceived as a characteristic of all social life, rather than as a roster of discrete units.

10. For example, from Kottak: "Anthropology is a uniquely *holistic* science of humanity" (1975, 3); from Plog and Bates: "The anthropological perspective, then, is *holistic*" (1976, 5); from Nanda: "anthropologists combine the study of both human biology and the learned and shared patterns of behavior we call culture. Other academic disciplines focus on one factor—biology, psychology, physiology, society. . . . Anthropology seeks to understand human beings as total organisms who adapt to their environments through a complex interaction of biology and culture. Because anthropologists have this 'holistic' approach to the study of the human experience, they are interested in the total range of human activity" (1987, 1); and from Ember and Ember: a "distinguishing feature of the discipline is its *holistic* or multifaceted approach to the study of human beings. . . . The discipline of anthropology retains its holistic orientation in that its many different specialties, taken together, describe many aspects of human existence, both past and present, on all levels of complexity" (1990, 3).

11. This "perception"—that introductory courses provide a vehicle for teaching the four-field model while more advanced courses generally do not—is more complex than it appears. It depends at once on the idea that the quadrants are more "specialized" than "general" anthropology and on the refusal to see the four-field model as something contestable, rather than something that needs to be the-

orized or that can be debated. Were the four-field ideal not given the status of orthodoxy, we would expect that anthropologists would feel compelled to offer advanced courses on it, to explore its strengths and weaknesses.

12. Segal (n.d.) argues that as a rule, pedagogic sequencing in modern schooling circulates most widely the most "mainstream" and hegemonic thinking, while placing both more formal and more unconventional thought into more restricted circulation.

13. Compare the institutionalized absence of intellectual debate between a course professor and her teaching assistant with Max Weber's (1958) comments on the desirability of having faculty with conflicting views co-teach so that students are not confronted with a single, authoritarian voice in the classroom.

14. To our knowledge, there has yet to be a careful examination of the history of the sequential reorganizations of the AAA. Though we have made no systematic comparison with other disciplines, it does appear that the AAA has gone through such "reorganization" more so than the associations of disciplines that might otherwise be seen as most comparable to anthropology (history and sociology, to give two examples). The reorganization of the early 1980s is recorded and narrated as a response to an adverse ruling of the Internal Revenue Service (IRS), though just why federal tax codes should have impacted so singularly on one discipline is an issue that is overlooked in these accounts. Moreover, it is not clear to us, from the standard recounting of these events, whether the reorganization of the 1980s was a *determining* cause of the departure from the AAA of many biological anthropologists or merely a precipitating event. There is no question in our minds, however, that this departure is part of the background of the subsequent fissuring of a small number of departments of anthropology at research universities, notably Duke and Stanford.

15. In no small part, we are thinking here of many of the public attacks on the editorial work of Barbara and Dennis Tedlock from 1994 to 1998. Some of these attacks were printed in the *Anthropology Newsletter*; others were voiced at AAA business meetings in those years.

16. The term *flagship* is wedded to the AA in the official discourse of the AAA; see, for example, www.aaanet.org/aa/, which we checked on June 2, 2004.

17. On the revolution in human time, see Stocking 1987; Trautmann 1987; Segal 2000.

18. Sahlins (1976) offers a fuller version of this argument about the autonomy of culture vis-à-vis biology. For related notions of hybrid phenomena, see Latour 1993.

19. One might add here that cultural-social anthropology is arguably the primary disciplinary home today for the practice of explicitly interpretive forms of social science. Thus to stifle this theoretical orientation within anthropology would be to leave the social sciences overall much less intellectually diverse.

20. It is important, we think, for anthropologists to keep in mind that significant critiques of scientific racism developed at roughly the same time outside of disciplinary anthropology, notably in the social-theoretical works of W. E. B.

Du Bois. See, in particular, chapter 6 of *Dusk of Dawn: An Essay toward an Autobiography of a Race Concept* (1940). On convergences, divergences, and the exchanges between Du Bois and Boas, particularly on race, see Liss (1998). On the relationship of Du Bois to anthropology and social theory more broadly, see Chandler 1996 and 2000.

21. Those within anthropology who perceive the bulk of contemporary cultural-social anthropology as not "scientific," and who present themselves as pursuing and seeking to organize in defense of "scientific anthropology," often assert that "science" is a result of following "*the* scientific method." Only rarely does this position engage the extensive literature in the philosophy and history of the sciences, which has debated whether there is any such thing as one "method" that produces "science."

22. Seizer (1995) speaks of anthropology as a "queer science," but Seizer does not herself locate this phrase in relation to the Kuhnian notion of "normal science"; and indeed, she has told one of us (Segal) that she was not explicitly thinking about Kuhn's work when she coined/deployed this phrase. Segal (1999) reframed Seizer's notion of a "queer science" in relation to Kuhn, however. As is well known, for Kuhn the contrast with "normal science" was not "queer science" but "scientific revolution." One might then say that we seek for anthropology a state of epistemological inquiry that Kuhn relegated only to the fleeting moments between variant normalcies. One can find Kuhn's notions in *The Structure of Scientific Revolutions* (1996 [1962]), which always bears rereading.

Rearticulating Anthropology

JAMES CLIFFORD

In *The Order of Things*, Michel Foucault argues that the modern disciplines, including anthropology, took shape during the nineteenth century in a discursive context where the figure of "man" had emerged as a complex subject and object of knowledge, simultaneously transcendent and empirical. I take this moment as a rough starting point for a discussion of how sociocultural anthropology makes and remakes itself in changing intellectual and institutional contexts. I write at a time of serious disagreement about whether we are at the end of the episteme Foucault identified—a set of assumptions under which "cultural" and "social" diversity across time and space can be construed as a describable and theorizable "human" inheritance. My approach, agnostic and metahistorical, leaves this and similar important disagreements unresolved while arguing that such disputes are constitutive of anthropology's shifting borders and intellectual alliances. I hope to describe a process of "disciplining" that is less about creating consensus than about managing dissent, less about sustaining a core tradition than about negotiating borders and constructing coalitions.

Invoking Foucault also recalls the embodied and institutional aspects of disciplinary formation. "Disciplining," as I understand it, is not only a matter of defining scholarly territories, research topics, and analytic methods—the "content" of a discipline. The term evokes older traditions of normative training and ascetic practice that take modern form in pastoral and governmental institutions, including the university. Disciplining is a process unfolding within these changing contexts. Anthropology is an academic practice unusually exposed to the post-1960s changes in perspective and political location associated with the linked phenomena of "decolonization" and "globalization." Modern anthropology, a comparative science of human diversity, was for its first century a "Western" science. This has begun, irreversibly, to change, along with the gendered, raced, and culturally conditioned bodies of its practitioners.

Elsewhere I have written about one aspect of this work-in-process, the normative function and professional habitus of "fieldwork," seen as a disputed, defended, and changing cluster of embodied practices (Clifford 1997b: 52–91). That discussion ends, like the current essay, with the prospect, but not yet the achievement, of "postcolonial" decentering. My concern is with institutional contexts of disciplining, especially zones of relationality, borderlands in which academic imagined communities routinely, creatively, and sometimes agonistically make and remake themselves. This approach extends what was postulated in the essay on fieldwork: a discipline most actively defines itself at its edges, in relation to what it says it is not. It does this by selectively appropriating and excluding elements that impinge, influences that must be managed, translated, incorporated. The process of incorporation also involves exclusion. A line is drawn in the interdisciplinary sand to mark a frontier. Something is taken in and something held at a distance, made "other." Over time, the line's position—contingent, policed, and transgressed—shifts tactically. This becomes apparent when one tracks anthropology's changing relations with history, with sociology, with literary studies, and with biology and evolutionary theories, to mention only some of the more well-traveled borderlands.

In an acute recent discussion, Virginia Dominguez explores the fraught and productive relationship of sociocultural anthropology with a new disciplinary alter ego, "cultural studies." Dominguez cites ten fundamental attitudes shared by anthropological and cultural studies work. She then demonstrates these overlaps in practice through an analysis of editorial board composition and articles published in two influential journals, *Cultural Anthropology* and *American Ethnologist* (both of which have abandoned "four-fields" coverage in favor of intensified links to social history, literary studies, Marxist analysis, race and gender studies, etc.). She then shows various tactics of disciplining that agonistically reestablish a sharp identity and sustain "a common presumption that Cultural Studies is 'other' to Anthropology" (1996, 46). At the current moment one can, in fact, observe a range of border attitudes, ranging from embattled "disciplinary patriotism" (Appadurai 1996, 29) to tactical, selective engagement to something close to a merging of horizons.

Sociocultural anthropology's self-image has long featured synthetic opportunism and openness to other disciplines. But too much engagement undermines a sense of integrity. Border crossing without policing erases the boundary. Thus even the most generous anthropological commentators on cultural studies are at pains to sustain at least a few key distinctions. For example, Richard Handler's review essay on the swiftly canonized and attacked collection *Cultural Studies* (edited by Grossberg, Nelson, and Treichler), cited by Dominguez (1996, 57), does not fail to argue for anthropology's more broad-ranging and analytically complex concept of "culture," as well as for its "trump card," ethnography. The significance of these two elements as distinguishing features of the discipline will appear below.

As Dominguez observes, the border work follows patterns analyzed by Fredrik Barth in his seminal volume, *Ethnic Groups and Boundaries* (1969). Disciplines, like ethnic groups, are subcultures of a wider polity—in this case, the university. They have no natural or autochthonous origin and must be articulated in situations of contact, overlap, and similarity. Populations, ideas, and practices routinely cross their borders and combine syncretically. For Barth, the sense of a group's distinction, its tradition or common culture, is always a secondary creation, not a primary cause or origin. Groups select certain traits with which they mark an identity, while trafficking among the many customs and practices they share with neighbors. In the community of sociocultural anthropologists, a fetishized practice of fieldwork has been used to sustain a professional distinction from qualitative sociology or cultural studies, marking off ideas and methods that might otherwise be indistinguishable. In other contexts, anthropology's purportedly unique local "contextualism," its "comparativism," or its "holism" have performed similar distinguishing work.

Barth observes that groups often show quite dramatic internal variety in their "ecological" adaptations while nonetheless sustaining a sense of common group identification through a selective marking of culture traits. Analogous niches in the interdisciplinary landscape are institutionalized by the sections of the American Anthropological Association, with their very different objects, languages, and research practices. What partial overlaps and tokens of recognition make them all "anthropologists," members of a group, as Barth puts it, who believe they are "playing the same game"? Rena Lederman (this volume) suggests that the American four fields, and until recently the requirement that graduate students take courses in at least three, contributed to a sense of solidarity. Indeed, the experience of a shared training may have been more important than any substantive ability to combine methodologies or fuse intellectual traditions.

In its normal functioning, a discipline does not actually need consensus on core assumptions. Rather like a hegemonic alliance, in Gramscian perspective, it requires consent, some significant overlapping interests, and a spirit of live-and-let-live across the differences. At times of crisis, such as the recent Tierney/Chagnon fracas (outlined below by Rena Lederman), a strong antagonism (of a "culture wars"/"science wars" variety) may divide the field. Divisions of this sort can lead to permanent splits in departments but seldom in the larger coalitional space of the discipline. Anthropology has, at least so far, managed to construct and reconstruct a hegemony from its contradictory elements. This is not to say that the elements remain the same. There is a constant coming and going, a realignment of interests and affiliations across changing interdisciplinary, institutional, and geopolitical terrains. In this perspective, the focus shifts away from identities to processes of identification. All disciplines, scientific and humanist, are diverse, actively self-defining communities. Thomas Kuhn (1996 [1962]) famously brought sociological consensus making, historicity, and the reinvention of traditions into the very heart of scientific practice (Phillips forthcoming). And recently Peter Galison (1997) has shown the discipline "physics" to be a trading zone of discrete subcultures (cited by Hodder in this volume). Indeed, Galison's theoretical and historical perspective may offer some useful insights to those who worry about anthropology's lack of a unified aim and method. Even the so-called "hard sciences" turn out to be rather loosely articulated. Building on these perspectives and on much other work in the historical sociology and ethnography of science, we can free ourselves from any assumption that "anthropology," always a confederation of traditions and practices, must strive for a unified identity modeled on a mistaken, ahistorical model of science.

Thinking about historical processes of identity formation, we focus on shifting domains of interdisciplinarity borderlands through which sharp borders are drawn and redrawn. Knowledge does not, of course, naturally sort itself out in professional segments, and institutionalized domains of academic practice are necessarily dynamic and relational. Thus I will be considering not only anthropology, but also some of its neighbors, trying to sketch a processual approach to disciplinary formation and change. My account is a partial one, focused largely on sociocultural anthropology in the United States and skewed toward the borderlands I know best, in the humanities and hermeneutic/historical social sciences. But I see no reason why the general approach should not apply to different national configurations of anthropology/ethnology or to other disciplinary boundaries—for example, those actively being renegotiated with biology, ecology, and the evolutionary and cognitive sciences.

Histories of institutionalization lean toward a functionalist analytic, constraining the innovative, productive dimensions of power Foucault always stressed. Thus I insist on processes of *disciplining*—the gerund evoking an ongoing, unfinished aspect. And I will be supplementing (not replacing) the Foucauldian account of governmentality with a more historically contingent and pragmatically political perspective signaled by the term *articulation*. My overview of anthropology and some of its neighbors is meant to be provocative, an incitation to step outside current polemics and reformist projects, attempts to recapture or redefine anthropology. My aim is to get a fresh perspective on interdisciplinarity, seen not as located *between* the disciplines—a misleading spatialization—but as inherent in the processes of connecting, disconnecting, and reconnecting organized domains of knowledge. Disciplining is always also interdisciplining.

"Articulation" suggests immediately the expressive, selective, and constructive process of speech. But most saliently here, it also refers to joints, connections, components of complex discursive/social bodies that can, with changing circumstances, be disarticulated. Stuart Hall explains:

> Articulation is a linkage which is not necessary, determined, absolute and essential for all time. You have to ask, under what circumstances *can* a connection be forged or made? So the so-called "unity" of a discourse is really the articulation of different, distinct elements which can be re-articulated in different ways because they have no necessary "belongingness." The "unity" which matters is a linkage between that articulated discourse and the social forces with which it can, under certain historical conditions, but need not necessarily, be connected (1996; 141).

Articulation theory, which Hall derives from Gramsci and Laclau, makes politically contingent the supposed necessity, determinism, or naturalness of social formations like "classes," "races," and "ethnicities." While the approach does not apply equally well to all sociocultural phenomena (some of which have deep local, historically sedimented roots), it certainly applies to those often fractious, recently formed communities, the academic disciplines.

During the early and mid-twentieth century, North American anthropology's distinctive "four fields" formed a persistent, if often unstable, historical bloc. The ensemble of overlaps and alliances sustaining this cultural, biological, archaeological, and linguistic academic tradition were, from the outset, recognized to be contingent and temporary by Franz Boas. The tradition's founder and exemplary practitioner had no illusions about any enduring unity of method or object, and indeed, he anticipated fissures and realignments in the immediate future (Boas 1904; discussed by Yanagisako this volume). He would have been astonished by the alliance's longevity (persisting rather like the Cheshire Cat from *Alice in Wonderland*—a body of shifting, differently copresent parts). If the four fields matrix has survived for a century after Boas's prediction, it is, George Stocking suggests (1988), because it has served at key times, such as the 1950s social science expansion, to characterize a healthy, capacious, scientific discipline for powerful university or governmental audiences. A kind of noble lie, perhaps. In fact, after Boas, no one has actually worked creatively in more than two of the four fields. And even Boas's exemplary contribution to all four fields is something of a myth, sliding rapidly over archaeology.

Perhaps the most dramatic disarticulation of the four fields ensemble has taken place with respect to "linguistic anthropology." Most departments today do not feel the need for a distinct linguistic track or faculty cluster. The study of linguistic process is very much part of anthropological work, but it tends to be seen as one of sociocultural anthropology's many provinces. Few anthropologists now study "languages" in the sustained descriptive/analytic way that was common to the generation of Sapir or Kroeber. As Silverstein argues (this volume), "Linguistic anthropology *is* sociocultural anthropology with a twist, the theoretical as well as instrumental (via 'discourse' or 'the discursive') worrying of our same basic data, semiosis in various orders of contextualization." Semiotic process, historicized (as in Silverstein's stress on creolization), names a rich domain of research that is arguably much closer to the concerns of cultural history than to those of much current linguistics. Indeed, the links with academic linguistics that were a major element in the relative autonomy of the linguistic subfield—epitomized in the figure of Sapir—have been loosened and in many areas severed. This is partly a result of the Chomskian revolution, which firmly realigned the linguistics mainstream with natural science. And it partly reflects the rise of semiology and a pervasive discursive turn in recent cultural analysis that has extended the domain of "the linguistic" beyond the Saussurian category of "language" (*langue*). This is to oversimplify a complex, uneven situation. But as William Foley has written in an explicit attempt at reconstruction, "Over the past few decades, linguistics and anthropology have increasingly diverged from each other, linguistics with a largely positivistic, structuralist orientation toward its subject matter and anthropology with a more interpretivist, discursive one, so that it is often difficult for specialists in the two fields to talk to each other. This has led to marginalization of anthropological linguistics in both disciplines" (1997, xiv). The legacies of "linguistic anthropology" (and "anthropological linguistics") are being pragmatically rearticulated in new interdisciplinary, institutional niches (e.g., Brenneis and Macaulay 1996; Foley 1997; Duranti 1997). What is not being rearticulated is a distinct and necessary fourth field of "anthropology."

Today, many more than four "fields," inside and outside institutional anthropology, cobble together active research domains. And this hyphenating diversity has characterized the range of "anthropological" activities at any historical moment. The normative vision of four fields resurfaces when members of the discipline feel called on to account for their collective identity, whether in a defensive or an entrepreneurial mode. Seen over time, collective identifications of this sort are inconsistent, aggressively asserted at times, negotiated and forgotten at others. The four-fields ideal has waxed and waned. In the years of shrinking resources following the 1950s and 1960s period of dramatic growth in the U.S. academy, a sense of lost direction and disciplinary crisis became more common. The four fields, which in the 1950s signaled an expansive and inclusive "science of Man," by the 1980s and 1990s came to represent a "back to basics" circling of the disciplinary wagons. Increased competition for resources is part of the story, as is the recent proliferation of interdisciplinary work in the humanities and interpretive social sciences (poststructuralism, neo-Marxist critical theory, semiotics, feminism) and in the natural sciences (hyphenated rearticulations of biology, the emergence of cognitive science, evolutionary psychology, and so on).

During the past two decades, a sense of disciplinary disarray has been in the air. Things fall apart. The center cannot hold. Mere cultural studies is loosed upon the world. Anthropology is not alone in feeling at sea. A few years ago, the Stanford Humanities Center organized a conference: "Have the Disciplines Collapsed?" The rhetoric of crisis, evoking loss of coherence, rigor, depth, and authority, tends toward the apocalyptic. But two recent historical studies of humanities disciplines, Gerald Graff's *Professing Literature* (1987) and Peter Novick's history of American historians, *That Noble Dream* (1988), dispel any idyllic memory of order and agreement *before* the current dissensus. Both works trenchantly argue, and illustrate in concrete detail, that disciplinary formation has always been a contingent, conflictual process. Graff describes literary studies as a long series of arguments about how "literature" should be understood and valued vis-à-vis historical context and theory. And he shows how fundamental, Arnoldian "humanist" values (themselves at one time fiercely resisted innovations) came to embody a kind of disciplinary ethos or common sense. Only relatively late, in the strongly contested postwar emergence of "New Criticism," did a method of close textual exegesis (similar in its normative function to fieldwork for anthropology and archival research for history) come to epitomize a disciplinary habitus. This innovation, now "traditional," is pitted against contemporary trends in literary or cultural theory, new historicism, postcolonial analysis, etc. And the cycle continues. Graff argues that disagreements about fundamental aims and methodologies are integral to the practice of organized literary study, conflicts that are more or less effectively managed through what he calls the "field-coverage principle" (1987, 6–8).

This principle was central to "the modernization and professionalization of education of the 1870s and 1880s, when schools and colleges organized themselves into departments corresponding to what were deemed to be the major subjects and research fields" (Graff 1987, 6). Disciplines were organized as a series of discrete territories worked on by specialists. If the basic fields were "covered," then so was the discipline. Graff argues that this mechanism allowed members of a discipline, in their everyday practice, to avoid, or bracket, fundamental arguments about goals and methods while still assuming that their diverse strategies would "add up." Since specialists enjoyed relative autonomy within their fields, research and pedagogy could be self-regulating. Moreover, organization by field coverage allowed academic disciplines to be flexible, and to absorb new approaches in an additive manner, by creating new fields. Initiatives that might address the fundamental, epistemological values of the discipline were thus included without causing changes across the whole array of fields. (For example, feminist anthropology could be added on, rather than anthropology becoming, significantly, feminist. See Marilyn Strathern's 1987 acute discussion of these issues.)

American anthropology's four traditional components, while they appropriate the normalizing disciplinary rhetoric of "fields," only partially correspond to Graff's description. They have, much of the time, allowed the cohabitation, without fundamental debate, of quite different research programs and practices (though tensions between natural scientific and historicist epistemologies have regularly surfaced and are currently hard to ignore, especially as competition for shrinking resources grows). Moreover, the four fields have difficulty functioning in a flexible, expansive managerial manner: the problem is the number four, which restricts additions yet does not reflect any widely shared understanding of structural/functional unity. In contrast, the field-coverage principle joins a vision of completeness to an open-ended series of specializations.

In practice, anthropology has worked through many proliferating and recombining interdisciplinary research alliances, and it has always been difficult to contain these articulations as subfields of cultural, archaeological, biological, and linguistic anthropology. At the departmental level, "fields" and "subfields," always quite selectively deployed, continue to function, producing local effects of wholeness and "coverage." But at a disciplinary level, these effects rely less on a gathering of fields, of whatever number, and more on a broader "disciplinary ensemble" (which I will sketch below), the basis for a traditional, transforming anthropological identity, both in America and elsewhere.

Peter Novick's (1988) critical history of the American historical profession offers many illuminating parallels with twentieth-century anthropology. Limiting myself to the postwar period, I underline his multidimensional account of what emerged after 1970 as a pervasive sense of crisis in the discipline. The 1950s and 1960s were boom years for American universities, and disciplines such as history and anthropology grew rapidly. The yearly conventions of the AAA and American Historical Association (AHA) (not to mention the omnibus Modern Languages Association [MLA]) turned into events without a core, increasingly massive agglomerations of subfields (Novick 1988, 580). Scale mattered: people began to lament a lost prewar sense of professional community when members from all parts of the discipline spoke to one another. After 1970 academic growth slowed dramatically, especially in nonscientific sectors, and historians were faced with a crisis of overproduction. Yet as career opportunities shrank, the discipline's range of subject matter and methodology continued to expand—from cliometrics to oral history, from the study of local parish registers to the world system, from feminism to urbanism, from material culture to media flows.

A sense of fragmentation and loss of direction was pervasive. In the 1970s and 1980s it was not only historians who felt their discipline no longer held together. Novick offers many quotations from distinguished historians that could apply equally well to anthropology or literary studies. For example, John Higham in 1985, discussing relations between Americanists and Europeanists in the U.S. profession, saw "a house in which inhabitants are leaning out of many open windows gaily chattering with the neighbors while the doors between the rooms stay closed" (quoted in Novick 1988, 578). A sense of disciplinary fragmentation (and, one might add, positive rearticulation) was compounded by rather fundamental disagreements about aims, methods, and epistemologies. History was going through its own "crisis of representation." Lawrence Veysey in 1979 was reduced to defining his field in minimalist terms: "All that unites historians is a concern for the evolution over time of whatever it is they study" (quoted in Novick 1988, 592). Clearly this is not enough to provide an adequate mark of distinction (in Barth's terms) for the profession, any more than saying anthropologists are defined by studying "culture" or literary scholars' "texts."

Novick takes his distance from the rhetoric of crisis in the 1970s and 1980s: "The bad news was that the American historical profession was fragmented beyond any hope of unification. The good news was that the fragments were doing very well indeed. New fields were explored in innovative ways: historical works of considerable originality and even brilliance appeared every year" (1988, 592). Something like this can no doubt be said about anthropology's unwrapped sacred bundle. But the problem of institutional identity remains. Disciplines are political/intellectual constructs. Exploring an analogy with nations, Novick (590) shows that the map of disciplines created in the late nineteenth century was not drawn up in any systematic way. The intellectual terrain was carved up agonistically and pragmatically by groups of scholars splitting off from older organizations and establishing discrete objects and methods. Over these claimed domains they asserted something like "sovereignty." But like national sovereignty, the borders established were in fact permeable, changing, in need of active management and selective policing. Novick's history amply supports an articulation approach to disciplinary process, allowing us to step back from perceptions of embattled traditions in crisis. Wary of all-or-nothing diagnoses, the approach does not confuse change with dissolution. Articulation assumes there is nothing necessary or determined about the academic professions—their defining fields, objects, methods, or borders. The disciplines were not always what they are now. They could be, will be, different.

Another example from the borders of anthropology poses instructive questions. Why is "geography" not an essential, core discipline in most U.S. universities? (Europe is another story.) There are, of course, geography departments, but these are quite unevenly distributed. Harvard, for example, got rid of geography in the early years of the century. Apparently the discipline is not like history or philosophy or physics, which no self-respecting university today can do without. One could imagine a university without a history department, where historical perspectives and methodology would be dispersed throughout the other disciplines. Indeed, a process like this seems to be under way in recent years (the emergence of "historical ethnography" in anthropology, of "new historicism" in literature). In some universities there are attempts to organize "historical studies" as an interdisciplinary cluster. One might even argue that something as important as "history" should never be the property of a limited group of professionals. (The same can be said about emergent formations—for example, "cultural studies" distinct from anthropology, "feminist scholarship" distinct from departments of "women's studies" or what is sometimes cobbled together these days under the title "visual culture.") But any imagined dispersal of history throughout the disciplines, even including the natural sciences, is utopic. While historical approaches can be found everywhere in the academic landscape, history proper is still considered to be a discrete territory, an essential discipline.

Why, compared to geography, is history, the study of past events, a more "essential" disciplinary formation? Why—to put it crudely—would a department of *time* be essential but not a department of *space*? A serious answer to this question would be complex and would need to confront in some detail the late-nineteenth-century contexts in which the modern disciplines were professionalized, a moment rather heavily burdened, as Nietzsche famously complained, by history (H. White 1978). It would also analyze the ideology of the "West" as a modernizing culture area, subject and object of a normative consciousness distinguishing it from exotic and backward "peoples without history" (Wolf 1982). And it would consider the connection of institutionalized historical scholarship with national projects. (Recent fights in Washington have been concerned with "*history* standards," where stories of national legitimation are at stake. It is hard to think of any issues in anthropology that could provoke similar arguments.) But whatever the reasons, history, not geography, remains an "intrinsic" discipline.

This may be changing. We are no longer positioned in the disciplines' formative late-nineteenth-century moment—when Western scholars could confidently sort out the spatio-temporal experiences of the rest of the world's societies along a continuum of separate cultures and a line of progress. Today, the changes designated by terms like *modernization* or *globalization* are no longer firmly oriented by a planetary map in which the West occupies the center and the others scramble to catch up from their various peripheries. Modernity has discrepant centers now, and the peripheries do not stay put. (Culturally and economically does California belong on the west coast of Euro-America, or on the eastern edge of the Asia-Pacific region?) In this new situation, a politicized, historicized geography is reemerging, articulated with a range of fields including urban studies, environmentalism, political economy, cultural anthropology, and feminism. It joins other composite disciplinary formations that analyze differently "located" forms of knowledge, culture, and indeed historical consciousness itself. The subaltern studies historian and critic Dipesh Chakrabarty (1992) calls this necessary, but by no means straightforward, process "provincializing Europe." Will the "givenness" of history as a discipline survive this open-ended transition? It will, in any event, need to renegotiate disciplinary borders with a revived and expansive geography (Gregory 1994).

One can ask similar questions about "literature" (until recently "English"). No doubt its traditional articulation with what Hall called "social forces"—such as Western civilizing projects, bourgeois marks of cultivation, or hegemonic national traditions—is a key source of its assumed necessity as a core discipline in the university. But parallel to history, its geopolitical location, the "Westernness" of its humanism, is increasingly at issue. So is its class identification with "high culture." There is no retreating from the dramatically expanded canon of the 1980s, its engagement with world literatures, with popular cultures, with visual and ethnographic modes. The coherence of literature, as topic and method, has loosened in a media age. It becomes necessary to ask why we still prescribe departments of literature and not of rhetoric or communication. An answer might begin with the eighteenth and nineteenth centuries and the displacement of rhetoric from its central place in the Western university curriculum. And we would have to reckon with a return of rhetoric and of the oral (including Walter J. Ong's "secondary orality") in academic configurations such as "popular culture," "oral literature," "communications," or "information." Indeed, the latter, as is now widely recognized, threatens to swamp the discrete identity of a textual corpus called "literature," turning it into a somewhat quaint, outdated site on the intercultural netscape. For example, Alan Liu's work analyzes and seeks to facilitate a transition in literature departments from producing "well-read" to "well-informed" citizens (see Liu 1998; 2004). Objects of study like "literature," which Foucault in *The Order of Things* shows emerging in the nineteenth century, may well be in the process of disappearance (or metamorphosis) at the beginning of the twenty-first.

We return to anthropology's own shifts and articulations. Detours through the related fields of geography, history, and literature have suggested a wider context for the current sense of a crisis in disciplinary identity, including all the defensive polemics that come with dis- and rearticulations of one's proper domain of knowledge. We feel, of course, that our own crisis is somehow more profound than anyone else's. American anthropology, while confronting its own special challenges (an extreme, public exposure to the contestations of decolonization, a rather sharp "two cultures" split), is very much part of the institutional, political, and intellectual transformations of the post-1970 U.S. academy.

Anthropology has long seen itself as bringing together disparate strands of knowledge. This is often celebrated as the field's special "holism," its ability to link science and the humanities, biology and culture, social structure and history. Anthropology's articulation of varied approaches has always been loose, however, creating a disjointed body sometimes stretched to the breaking point. How has the discipline kept from falling apart? What elements, in the twentieth century, have remained more or less firmly glued together, components of a persistent, distinctively "anthropological" tradition?

The U.S. four fields no longer supply, if they ever did, a rigorous intellectual map. And at the level of socialization, of graduate training, their ideal of coverage is more often than not honored in the breach. Seen comparatively, they are at best a local articulation. Elsewhere, anthropology has taken quite different shapes. In Europe, archaeology is quite reasonably associated with history, and there is no prescriptive connection between sociocultural and biological anthropology. (In the French tradition *ethnologie* has been clearly distinct from *anthropologie*, and Lévi-Strauss's influential appropriation of the latter term was more philosophical than biological.) This is not to say, of course, that there are no substantial commonalities or overlaps among the various "anthropological" traditions. It is, however, to argue that these do not add up to a rational program or a clearly definable intellectual project. The "wholeness" of the twentieth-century discipline has, rather, depended on a loosely articulated discursive and institutional formation, a common sense that has recently become visible as it has come under pressure from all sides.

A rough overview of this common sense (always susceptible to local versions and exceptions) would replace the American "four fields" with four theoretico-practical disciplinary components. During the first three quarters of the twentieth century the professional community of anthropologists managed to agree, most of the time, on (1) an empirical object, (2) a distinctive method, (3) an interpretive paradigm, and (4) a telos or transcendent object. The object was "primitive" societies; the method was "fieldwork"; the paradigm was "culture"; the telos was "Man."

(1) The discipline's common empirical *object* was "primitive," archaic, non-Western, non-"modern" societies. The emphasis is clear in Boas's often-cited 1904 definition, which linked "the biological history of all mankind" to "linguistics applied to people *without* written languages; the ethnology of people *without* historic records; and *pre*historic archaeology" (Boas 1904, 35; emphasis added). A "division of knowledges," as Michèle Duchet (1984) calls it in her study of the eighteenth-century

origin of this specialization, separated anthropology/ethnology from history/sociology. Human societies, objects of study, were divided into us and them. This specialization deepened in the nineteenth century, as essentialist concepts of race and culture took hold. Thus, in its formation as a discrete perspective, anthropology was enmeshed in colonialist ideological structures (however anticolonialist its content may at times have been). The marking off of its special object reinforced common distinctions between societies with and without history or writing, simple versus complex, cold versus hot, traditional versus modern. Anthropology filled in the details of an expansionist Europe's "savage slot" (Trouillot 1991). And it peopled the world with "other cultures," sometimes seen as earlier civilizational stages, sometimes as synchronically dispersed samples, of humanity.

(2) Primitive or exotic peoples could become empirical, closely studied scientific objects because scholars could travel to study them in distinctly anthropological ways. The twentieth-century discipline's characteristic *method*, participant-observation fieldwork, though it had older roots, was given normativity by the Malinowskian generation. What emerged was an unstable but productive fusion of objective and subjective methods (sometimes evoked as both a laboratory and a rite of passage). This "deep" form of experiential/analytic, hermeneutic/scientific research became a defining feature of anthropology—even though it was, in fact, generally limited to the sociocultural branch and even there practiced rather unevenly. The history of what counts as adequate fieldwork shows great variation in length and nature of visiting/dwelling; relative mastery of language(s); rise and decline of scientific methods like kinship description and political conditions of research, etc. But through all its transformations, anthropological fieldwork sustained, against neighboring disciplines such as sociology or economics, the norm of a peculiarly intensive and interactive research methodology. Moreover, the discipline's general identification as a "field science" may have been critical in determining the articulation of archaeology to anthropology (particularly in expansive, settler-colonial national contexts) (Trigger 1984).

(3) Anthropology's interpretive *paradigm* was "culture," or, in more Durkheimian traditions, "the social." Well-worn arguments between British and American anthropologists over the relative merits of "culture" and "social structure" take place within the general paradigm. I am referring to the closure produced by describing a culture, a cultural way of life, a

society, or a social structure. (Thornton 1988 offers a trenchant critique of such taxonomic reifications.) Culture—always shadowed by its agonistic/synergistic double, "race"—has been an enormously productive and elastic concept. For much of the twentieth century, the discipline of anthropology claimed a kind of eminent domain over one of its major meanings (relativistic ways of life/arrangements of "learned" human behavior). Culture and its surrogates functioned as a "paradigmatic tradition," to adopt Stocking's (1992b) version of Kuhn. It gave everyone in the discipline an understanding of what the common problem was, what the form was whose blanks needed filling in. Recurring disputes over the proper understanding of nature versus nurture, evolutionary versus social-historical components of human behavior, were built into the paradigm. For "culture" denoted both structured, separate ways of life *and* what humans had that animals did not ("Man the culture-bearing animal" was a commonplace). "Culture" finessed the deep epistemological division between (biological) evolutionary and historicist explanations for patterns of behavior. Structural notions of language—Saussure's *langue/langage*, the former designating specific languages, the latter a general human capacity—did the same double work. (Silverstein, this volume, explores the breakdown of this paradigm, which he associates with antiprocessual "taxonomic" and "museological" impulses.)

(4) Finally, the discipline's *telos*, "Man," might best be called a transcendent object, since it is not like primitive, exotic societies, something assumed to be "out there" that one can visit and study. "Man" functioned more as ultimate horizon for an anthropology that, for a century or so, defined itself as the "science of man" (Marcel Mauss's *homme total*). Everything anthropology did could be understood to contribute to knowledge of this figure. I use the term *figure* in its rhetorical sense of symbolic condensation. The figure of Man, in the nineteenth century, was profoundly temporal. Organicist assumptions, common to notions of cultural and biological "life," combined with historical/evolutionary models of development to undergird a pervasive modern common sense, a set of assumptions that, as Sylvia Yanagisako (this volume) makes clear, are still with us, though under new pressure. This is the epistemic territory of Foucault's "Man," the empirical/transcendental double analyzed in *The Order of Things*. A potent figure was underwritten, in disciplinary anthropology, by the elastic "culture" paradigm, by the simultaneously experiential and scientific practice of fieldwork, and by a global setup in which

any society (however "savage" or "simple") could stand as an empirical instance of a developing humanity, a collectible, classifiable piece of a puzzle. Ethnography, archaeology, history, physical anthropology, and linguistics were all part of this overall project. The teleological figure of "Man," whether conceived in evolutionist or taxonomic terms (in practice, usually some combination of the two), was projected from a site of theorization firmly situated in a transcendent "modern" West. While Foucault does not feature this specifically colonial foreshortening, it becomes inescapable when considering late-twentieth-century postcolonial challenges to anthropology's telos.

This disciplinary ensemble—combining a distinctive object, method, paradigm, and telos—no longer looks as natural as it once did. Every element is actively contested. Yet it would be utopian and ahistorical to claim that it is now finished, that some whole new formation is emerging. Rather an accelerated series of shifts and realignments seems to be under way between the discipline's subfields and across its many external borderlands. Each of the four disciplinary components mapped above has come in for strong critical scrutiny, followed by ("baby/bathwater") agendas of rescue, redefinition, and recombination. The four components persist, no longer linked by a disciplinary "common sense" but reconceived and reconnected in partial, tactical ways. I offer not a map, but some signs of current rearticulation.

(1) *Object.* Anthropologists no longer specialize in "primitive" societies. They "study up," in Laura Nader's famous phrase (1969), and the range of sociocultural contexts that can be treated "anthropologically" is potentially vast: from country clubs to computer hackers, from tourist performances to physics labs, from soundscapes to video productions, from traveling African musicians to Melanesian *kastom* movements. Of course, this expanded, even promiscuous, range compounds long-standing problems of disciplinary definition. In particular, the constitutive oppositions with sociology and history, based on a now-apparent colonial specialization, have broken down. Anthropologists no longer prescriptively study "out" and "down." Moreover, anthropologists' former objects—small-scale, tribal, subaltern, and out-of-the-way peoples—are recognized as having been actively engaged with precolonial and colonial histories and as possessing distinct forms of historical consciousness. Anthropol-

ogy's former objects are now repositioned as coeval participants in systems of differently "globalizing" economic, sociocultural power. (Among the many who have contributed to these developments: Rosaldo 1980; Dening 1980; Fabian 1983; Sahlins 1985.)

This displacement of anthropology's long-naturalized site of specialized overview—looking "out" and "back" from the end or cutting edge of a progressive history—has involved ongoing renegotiations of boundaries, roles, and methods. The title of a recent collection of contemporary sociocultural work, *Exotic No More* (MacClancy 2002), proclaims, a bit defensively, the new orientation. At the same time, for many in the discipline, the former emphasis on the exotic and the marginal remains a valued, defining feature, albeit in need of postcolonial reconception. What other academic discipline attends, as anthropology has, to the experiences of marginal and voiceless peoples? I argue elsewhere (Clifford 2000) that sociocultural anthropology has characteristically made, and should continue to make, two crucial interventions, asking: "What else is there?" and "Not so fast!" Both questions are tied to the discipline's brief for diversity, its sense that there are more things in heaven and earth than are dreamt of in general theories of evolution or globalization. A legacy of anthropological exoticism, at its best a form of lucid, intense attention to otherness, is still part of the anthropological habitus. It is sometimes claimed that anthropology is distinctively "comparative" in its worldview. Of course, more or less explicit comparison is a characteristic of all critical thought, and anthropology's more successful comparative topoi (the gift, kinship, the person) are not inherently different from phenomena understood comparatively by other human sciences. What remains distinctive is the scope of comparison, the range of sociocultural phenomena in large and small sites, that anthropology finds it necessary to consider. (In this egalitarian agenda it most closely resembles, perhaps, linguistics, for which there are no important and unimportant languages.)

(2) *Method.* The disciplinary template for proper fieldwork is contested and complicated from several directions: new forms of reflexivity, the projects of "indigenous" scholars, and the proliferation of "ethnographic" approaches across the human sciences and humanities. There is no need to belabor the fact that "the field" is not what it used to be (e.g., Rabinow 1977; Tsing 1993; Gupta and Ferguson 1997). Some anthropologists struggle to contain these changes, seeing only epistemological jitters and a

dangerous politicization. Others (myself included) find the glass half full, hoping for a thorough decolonization of research and a rebirth of hermeneutically sophisticated ethnography.

Whatever the uneven results of the changes under way, an anthropological style, distinctive in the current interdisciplinary jumble of "ethnographic" methods, is still relatively clear. A good deal of effort has recently been exerted to sharpen this disciplinary borderline, especially vis-à-vis more "literary" or "cultural studies" approaches. Depth and interactivity of research, guaranteed by revised notions of dwelling, alliance, language competence, translation, and hermeneutic process, remain characteristic of "anthropological" ethnography. Traditions of "fieldwork," delinked from histories of exotic travel, colonial governmentality, and class paternalism, are newly entangled in the "complex connectivity" (Tomlinson 1999) and power-charged countercurrents too quickly rounded up by the term "globalization."

In these worldly contexts, anthropological ethnography offers its indispensable complicating message: "Not so fast!" The bottom-up, peripheral histories it renders; the attention to local-level pragmatics, to surprising outcomes (for example, the inventive cultural survival of many supposedly doomed tribal peoples)—all contribute to Marshall Sahlins's (2000b) "anthropological enlightenment." The challenge is to make these "ethnographic" interventions something more than nominalist ("Two Crows Denies It") objections in the interdisciplinary, comparative study of global processes. Thus the particularist localism of much traditional fieldwork is being reconceived—for example, in Anna Tsing's (1993) account of a complexly connected "out-of-the-way place" or George Marcus's (1995) conception of "multisited" ethnography.

(3) *Paradigm.* "Culture," generally understood as either discrete, historical systems of meaning and practice or as an evolutionary capacity to learn and transmit behavior, has been appropriated and rearticulated by a range of other disciplines in the humanities and the evolutionary/cognitive sciences. Culture can no longer be defined in a rigorously "anthropological" way (if it ever could; Kroeber and Kluckhohn 1952). Yet what is still often referred to as the "anthropological culture idea" (relativist, small "c") is ubiquitous across the humanities and human sciences, despite recurring attempts to cut it down to size. In this situation, anthropology appears to be a victim of its own success. "Culture" has become what Roland Barthes once called a "mana word." People routinely evoke the

"culture" of corporate executives, the military, teens, medieval villages, Balinese, chimpanzees, the Internet. Anthropology's once distinctive paradigm now underwrites a vast range of work in many fields.

While the concept of culture cannot provide a central paradigm for contemporary anthropology, it remains a critical stake, what W. B. Gallie (1964) might call an "essentially contested" disciplinary category. A recent Wenner Gren symposium brought together a representative range of anthropological scholars to assess the status of the concept, and—in the words of its organizers—to move "beyond culture worry." In their introduction to the substantial and diverse collection of essays that emerged from the symposium, Richard Fox and Barbara King (2002) argue that disciplinary vitality depends on separating anthropology from its too close association with the culture paradigm: "We need not be locked into one view of anthropology in the same way we once asserted that 'the natives' were locked into their cultures" (19). Fox and King see anthropology as polymorphous and opportunistic, working with an open-ended range of methodologies, theories, and objects of study. Indeed, the quite various, sometimes contradictory, views of "anthropology beyond culture" represented by the twelve collected essays confirm this sense of multiplicity.

The book's editors are not overly concerned about the discipline's soul or identity. Looking beyond the "culture worry" that they find in the work of Geertz and Ortner ("among many others") in Sahlins's aggressive defenses of culture, and in attempts "to invalidate anthropology" by unnamed "critics" (no doubt pesky postmodernists), Fox and King affirm "an abiding commitment to anthropology as *the comprehensive study of humankind (including our near primate relatives)*" (2002, 19; my emphasis). Lest one suspect this rather breathtaking ambition might be casual rhetoric, they go on to specify: "The breadth of anthropology—whether that breadth be measured by its coverage of the world's peoples, its historical depth, or the variety of its ethnographic, comparative, evolutionary, and developmental analyses—is unmatched by other scholarly disciplines" (19).

Some will be unsure whether this evokes a potentially coherent "comprehensive study of humankind" or a discipline splitting apart, spread too thin. At the very least, it suggests anthropology's current state of what might be called loose articulation. "Culture" variously defined—attacked, defended, inflated, cut back, bypassed—remains in the mix but no longer at the center. Often it is deployed in loose adjectival or compound forms: "cultural politics," "the culture industry," "diaspora culture," "youth subcultures." The concept is clearly too important and pervasive to reject or replace. Yet its paradigmatic disciplinary function, as Fox and King recognize, has been undermined or, better, dispersed. "Culture" is all over the place. And the different ways it is understood by historical ethnographers, textual critics, or neo-Gramscian political analysts have little in common with its uses by most evolutionary theorists or cognitive scientists.

(4) *Telos*. The figure of "Man" (or its current improved version, "humanity") seems more and more blatantly a rhetorical condensation of disparate elements. Foucault and feminism have chased "Man" from the masthead of most anthropological journals. (*L'Homme* is the last hold-out.) But if the masculinist signifier is disappearing, we are far from the "posthumanist" world imagined by a generation of radical poststructuralists. Man/humanity remains a potent vision, something to speak for, to reach for, to grasp in as comprehensive a manner as possible. Recently I heard the dean of humanities at my university, Wlad Godzich, argue forcefully that the development and diverse possibilities of "the human" were the proper domain of "the humanities." (He was probably including at least sociocultural anthropology and historical archaeology in this somewhat imperial claim.) But no doubt other discourses, based in evolutionary biology, philosophy, linguistics, or cognitive science, could make the same kind of statement appropriating the human.

Anthropologists can still be heard talking of their discipline's special dedication to understanding "human behavior" (as if this distinguished it from history, literature, philosophy, sociology, etc.). But, of course, when anthropology—at least in its American vein—called itself "the science of man," it was not claiming to study everything human. It was asserting a specific holism, an array of concerns including current sociocultural life, the archaeological past (historic and prehistoric), primate and early hominid evolution, and the varieties of language use. And as we have seen, the range of human societies and histories condensed in this science was limited. It was generally understood that anthropology's "man" was limited to peoples (primitive/exotic or small-scale) whose societies and/or cultures could be studied holistically; to ancient, premodern, non-Western histories; to human and primate evolution. The focus was overwhelmingly on early and non-Western humanity. Thus, in practice, the ultimate goal and horizon, "Man," was foreshortened, made real, by a disciplinary ensemble composed of a limited object, method, and paradigm. As the identity of this ensemble loosens, anthropology becomes, more than ever, a changing field of discrepant and overlapping alliances.

Since the 1960s, anthropology's defining elements have been thoroughly rearticulated. The contributions in this volume offer many examples of broken links and new connections. This is not to say that earlier disciplinary formations were misguided or did not produce valuable, concrete knowledge. It is only to argue that the disciplining and interdisciplining of anthropological knowledge and research practices are productive and ongoing. Anthropology has always been cobbled together, constructed from disparate influences, humanistic and scientific. It is worth remembering that none of the discipline's founders (trained in physics, medicine, biology, history, philology, sociology, religious studies, *sciences coloniales*, missions) were "anthropologists." And during the past century the moments of disciplinary consensus have never gone unchallenged. To mention only one example among many: Radcliffe-Brown's postwar program of a "natural science of society" was almost immediately punctured by Evans-Pritchard's famous defection to history in 1951.

The discipline of anthropology seems currently to be in an accelerated, "hot" moment of rearticulation. It seems unlikely, however, that anthropology departments will shortly disappear—if only for reasons of institutional inertia, but also because "anthropological perspectives," if not easily defined, are widely recognized and valued. Some departments may take new, hyphenated names or add specifying adjectives. And in this they more resemble contemporary sciences like biology, which quite regularly recombine and split, than the purportedly essential disciplines of the traditional "arts and sciences" university. Indeed, in the general approach I have been proposing, even the best established canonical traditions are seen to have been constituted and reconstituted in practice through interdisciplinary articulations and disarticulations,

It is important, of course, to distinguish disciplines from individual departments. If the former are "imagined communities," their communal mode of government can be quite loosely federal. Witness the capacious programs for the annual meetings of the AAA, the MLA, the Linguistic Society of America, or the AHA. Particular departments reflect more specific arrangements: ruptures, struggles, truces, reinventions of local tradition and community. Few pretend to cover the whole disciplinary landscape. In the San Francisco Bay Area, Stanford and u.c. Berkeley offer an interesting contrast. The former recently opted for a segmentary solution (hiving off "cultural and social anthropology," linked with interpretive archaeology, from "anthropological sciences"). The latter formally maintains four fields but in practice seriously supports only two, the sociocultural and archaeological, themselves diverse and ramifying. (In this case, linguistic anthropology becomes effectively an element of the sociocultural area, distant from many current developments in linguistics.) Stanford's "cultural and social" formation resembles that of other major departments—for example, Chicago, Princeton, and Duke ("cultural" separate from "biological anthropology and anatomy"). Indeed, the widespread rapprochement of sociocultural and historical approaches suggests a new version of the "ethnology" that Robert Lowie, in his *History of Ethnological Theory* (1937), preferred to "anthropology." In this development, sectors of American anthropology realign themselves with historically oriented European versions of the discipline (especially in Germany, Central Europe, and Scandinavia). Archaeology, by definition a "historical" science, is divided over whether its basic approach should be (scientific) evolutionist or (interpretive) historicist. Recent trends in the United States and Britain point in generally opposite directions (Gosden 1999, 8), with room for a range of specific alliances, such as that forged by Ian Hodder and his colleagues at Stanford (this volume).

These are only some of the currently active dis- and rearticulations of American anthropology. Moreover, the sociocultural emphasis of the departments mentioned above does not exclude productive relations across the sometimes fraught lines separating biology and culture, evolution and history, positivism and hermeneutics—battlegrounds in the recent "science wars." One might note Emory University's commitment to holism, linking especially cultural and biological agendas, or u.c. San Diego's similar scope, with a special emphasis on psychological approaches. Work in archaeology and linguistic anthropology bridges humanistic and scientific epistemologies in specific projects. In others, researchers align themselves with one or the other of the "two cultures." For example, the University of Chicago program, makes no commitment to knowledge of "the human" or to archaeology and biological anthropology. The departmental website, quite unlike Emory's, eschews holistic claims and simply advertises the current research emphases of faculty, mostly on contemporary historical and sociocultural problems—research that connects directly with work in allied disciplines.

Anthropology's range of extramural articulations is very wide. Links between social historians and historical ethnographers; between feminist anthropologists and women's studies; between cognitive anthropology and psychology; between archaeology and biology, art history, or classics, etc. are achieved through specific alliances in and across hyphenating programs. They cannot be understood as elements of an assumed disciplinary identity or prescriptive tradition. The processes of (inter)disciplining, making and unmaking an articulated ensemble called anthropology, are ordinary activities that cannot be contained by periodic "back to basics" reactions. The "basics" are, of course, selections in new circumstances from among the tangled resources of tradition.

In the approach I have been outlining, perceptions of crisis (and renewal) register normal disciplinary realignments in conflictual and creative institutional contexts. Readers may legitimately wonder if this kind of analysis is troubling or reassuring, enlightening or irrelevant. It does not identify the ongoing core, the soul, of anthropology, nor does it offer much advice for charting the discipline's immediate course. In the longer term, anthropology may well come to be understood as a "twentieth-century" science, its ideas, objects, and methods subsequently redistributed in other academic constellations. Or it may be that segments of the traditional discipline will become, like geography, important fields of knowledge unevenly present in restructured American universities. Or, as Lederman hopes, anthropology may persist as a polythetic cluster, an opportunistic, loose coalition of approaches, that sustains itself in the shifting intellectual/institutional landscape by contributing a distinctive breadth of comparative approaches, an openness to humanist/scientific crossovers, and an ethnographic commitment to "local knowledge" (Geertz 1983).

The above account offers no answers for immediate dilemmas of articulation raised throughout this volume. It skirts the important question of anthropology's public reputation, an issue sometimes condensed in the desire for a "new Margaret Mead." Nor does it address the important issue of how disciplinary fronts can be tactically sustained in contexts of budget shortfalls and administrative downsizing. Indeed, I have focused rather narrowly on academic matters, without considering broader changes that exert structural pressures on current rearticulations. Two immediately come to mind: (1) the ongoing, and unfinished, decolonization of a Euro-American–centered science of man and culture, something I have discussed elsewhere (e.g., Clifford 1997b) but here mention only in passing; and (2) the neoliberal corporate university, with its increased emphasis on marketable outcomes, flexible research teams, and audit-driven interdisciplinarity. In the sometimes brutal readjustments of the contemporary university, it may be important to resist managerial trends by defending traditional disciplinary spaces. But the history of disciplining and articulation I have been sketching makes it clear that such defensive postures can be sustained only at risk of irrelevance and sclerosis.

Unchosen Grounds
Cultivating Cross-Subfield Accents for a Public Voice

RENA LEDERMAN

We are not the only discipline to be arguing about the conditions making possible our intellectual future. At its 2001 annual meeting in Snowmass, Colorado (as elsewhere these days), for example, the international high-energy physics community fielded proposals for the next-generation particle accelerator (Glanz 2001). Alternative proposals reflected different senses if not of what the fundamental questions are, then just how distant a horizon to aim for. Quite a bit was at stake since, at a cost of $6 billion or so, only one of these machines can be built. Despite significant disagreements, particle physicists at the laboratories, universities, and institutes of many countries perceived a need to speak with one voice about significance and feasibility to persuade policy makers and publics in the United States and elsewhere about funding the project. The changing geopolitical economy of high-energy physics—the prototypical "big science" but "no longer the favorite son," as one meeting participant put it (Seife 2001)—required such pragmatics both at pivotal public moments like this and in the work-aday conduct of research (where single experiments often involve international collaborations of hundreds of scientists and technicians).

Not so for the social sciences and humanities. Thomas Kuhn's confrontation with "unanticipated problems" concerning differences between the natural scientists with whom he was familiar and the social scientists he came to know in 1958–1959, during his stay at the Center for Advanced Studies in the Behavioral Sciences, prompted him to recognize the role of normalizing research "paradigms" specifically in the natural sciences (1970 [1962], vii–viii; see also 209 and elsewhere). The contrast may be overdrawn.[1] It is nevertheless clear that, at least in anthropology and related fields, a lack of normalization—sharp internal differences concerning both substance and method and a historically shifting dialectic of interdisciplinary border crossing and disciplinary border policing—is perfectly normal (as James Clifford, this volume, reminds us; see also, e.g., Gieryn 1999; Klein 1996; Silverstein this volume). In this steeply contoured terrain we locate our questions about the organization of our knowledge production and its specific situational pragmatics.

Daniel Segal and Sylvia Yanagisako have focused our attention on one significant question of this sort: the contested status of anthropology's "sacred bundle" (Stocking 1988) of four subfields with respect to the discipline's identity and intellectual effectiveness. They have suggested that "unwrapping" the bundle might mean exploring the discipline's institutional history and relations with other disciplines. Taking their cue about the need for a broad context, I argue that our disagreements about the subfields are part of a rift that is not confined to anthropology, nor even to academic discourse. This fault line, which cleaves essentialist and contextualizing ways of knowing, runs through American culture.[2] While it is most certainly evident in conflicts *among* anthropological subfields (notably cultural and biological anthropologies), it can also be found *within* each subfield and shows up, as well, in many interdisciplinary and entirely nonacademic contexts. Conversely, cultivating cross-subfield accents—identifying affinities and openings that make strategic cooperation possible among the subfields—has been, and may continue to be, anthropology's distinctive disciplinary resource for addressing important scholarly and public issues.

To identify the underlying issues, I will focus in some detail on my own subfield of sociocultural anthropology. I will use one of the larger discipline's constitutive practices—cross-cultural comparison—as an initial lens through which we might view the sociocultural version of this dialectic.[3]

"Two Cultures" (after a Fashion)
within Sociocultural Anthropology

Along with fieldwork (face-to-face engagement with social actors) and attention to the taken-for-granted conditions of everyday life (its tacit constructions, conventions, and practices), a comparative perspective has historically defined sociocultural anthropology's complementary value relative to neighboring disciplines, not to mention its public cachet. On one hand, we have used comparison to make "cultures" (as socially meaningful orderings of experience) visible, ethnographically and otherwise. On the other hand, comparison has driven and qualified anthropology's distinctively thematic (or theory-driven) regionalism, distinguishing it from the unqualified regionalism of area studies programs (Lederman 1998). What is more, as one of the distinctive features of its twentieth-century practice—constituting its identity and sensibility—comparativism does not belong to sociocultural anthropology alone but informs all four subfields one way or another. Although it is a tacit condition of much anthropological work, comparativism becomes evident, at the least, as a means by which anthropology is understood to make a complementary contribution relative to other fields (see, e.g., Calhoun 2002, 3). A comparative perspective is explicitly articulated in the subfields' respective engagements with their more parochical inter- and extradisciplinary interlocutors.

Nevertheless, within sociocultural anthropology, the "hows" and the "whys" of cross-cultural comparison have been contested throughout the last century (see, e.g., Holy 1987a for several very useful essays).[4] Twentieth-century sociocultural anthropology has had two important styles of comparative analysis: positivist and interpretive. They are our local version of "the two cultures." In his influential and extensively criticized essay by that name, C. P. Snow (1993 [1959]:4) developed a distinction between the (physical) sciences and (literary) humanities. While I have no interest in adopting Snow's position here (e.g., his castigation of "literary intellectuals" for their putative pessimism, elitism, and ignorance of science), my aim is to adopt the "two cultures" tag as an alternative to the more recent "science wars" (Gross and Levitt 1994; Ross 1996; Damasio et al. 2001; see Gieryn 1999 for a useful review). I use the tag, with qualifying quotation marks, to suggest a complex oppositional relation between knowledge practices: "cultures" indeed, although not in Snow's "common attitudes" sense (9), but rather with the contemporary implication of unbounded, relationally self-defining, unstable, internally heterogeneous constructs. All qualifications aside, Snow's central concern with the *public reception* of increasingly specialized knowledge is a key theme for me in this essay.[5]

Snow's tag usefully captures the popular simplification that also affects our own thinking. The sciences and humanities are too often represented as either simply irreconcilable (e.g., Gross and Levitt 1994) or unproblematically complementary (Bernard 1994, 1–18). Both positions are both real and partial. In practice, positivist and interpretive approaches are mutually implicated in a tangled skein of hierarchies, conflicts, and compatibilities with regard to their modes of engaging and representing the world (e.g., Biagioli 1999; Gieryn 1999). Both the tangles and their impatient simplifications are what make their insinuation in and around anthropological debates so problematic.

Scientific (objectivist) comparative anthropology—exemplified by the Human Relations Area Files (e.g., Murdock 1971), materialist (e.g., Harris 1968), and sociobiological (Chagnon 1983) anthropologies (but evident also in some versions of structural, ecological, Marxian, and psychoanalytic work)—is a diverse and mutually contestatory set. Accepting the need for a language of observer-defined categories that can be used consistently across cultural contexts, this family of comparativist styles makes an analytical distinction between observer and observed (often referred to as "etic" and "emic" perspectives; e.g., Harris 1968; Bernard 1994). It foregrounds cross-cultural similarities, taking them as evidence of formal, functional, or developmental (cultural-evolutionary) relations about which universal definitions, law-like generalizations, or statistical regularities can be discerned. From this standpoint, the second comparative style can appear non- or even anticomparative (e.g., Köbben 1970; Holy 1987a).[6]

The second family of comparativist styles includes an equally diverse array of interpretive, symbolic, and reflexive approaches (including other versions of structural, ecological, Marxian, feminist, and psychoanalytic work). Heirs to Boasian "historical particularism" and other traditions inside anthropology and out (e.g., Evans-Pritchard 1965; Geertz 1973; see also Dresch et al. 2000; Fardon 1990; Peel 1987), these styles privilege the understanding of particular cultural and historical contexts.[7] While practitioners are attentive to structural inequalities of power and knowledge, they take human realities to be a play of positioned, contingent perspectives—always potentially contestable, no matter how durable in practice. Observer-defined terms tend to be unstable since the observer/observed distinction is relativized in significant ways. Attending to the meanings informing social action, this comparativist stance tends to foreground cultural differences (rather than similarities) and is particularly sensitive to situational translation problems (e.g., Strathern 1981, 1989; Boon 1998). For example, Renato Rosaldo identifies a "near paradox, the simultaneous specification/comparison goal of Clifford Geertz's essays" (1999, 32), a goal that acknowledges the literal untranslatability of local constructs in the very act of conveying their cross-cultural intelligibility. Rosaldo invokes Geertz's demonstration that socially engaged witnessing of unfamiliar cultural enactments (of distinctively Javanese bereavement in this instance) enables one "to take the possibility of such a conception . . . seriously and appreciate, however inaccessible it is to you, its own sort of force" (34, quoting Geertz).

A similar globally framed specificity is evident in the past thirty years' increasingly historical and culturally alert work on relations among colonialism, racism, sexuality, and gender (e.g., Cooper and Stoler 1997; Jolly 1993) and in the now pervasive attention to transnational political, economic, and cultural relations (e.g., Fox 1991; Hannerz 1996; Marcus 1995; Sahlins 1985). Because of its tendency to obviate the observer/observed distinction, this style of comparison is itself ethnographic and historical (Peel 1987, 88). It deemphasizes the simply analytical juxtaposition of cultures, the "armchair exercise" of reading ethnography and deriving functional or causal relationships from the study of cultural units treated as closed systems or functional wholes. Instead it foregrounds intercultural conjunctures—historical and contemporaneous instances of exchange, domination, exclusion, and violence—deriving insight from the parallel, divergent, or conflicting senses that differently positioned social actors make of events (e.g., Sahlins 1981; see also Sewell 1999 and, for important qualifications, Marcus 1999b).

As with other variants of the "two cultures," the relationship between this pair of comparative styles is complex, ambivalent, and not simply antagonistic. On one hand, they are mutually complementary insofar as both contribute to anthropology's history of "cultural critique" (Marcus and Fischer 1986). Each has deployed its own kind of comparison to debunk or to qualify familiar Euro-American ideas about culture and history, including unremarked hints of Euro-American folk categories flavoring the specialist knowledges of our academic neighbors like economics, philosophy, psychology, or biology (Ingold 1996a, 1–2). The point is that depending on the circumstances, either comparativist argument— "We're essentially similar, however distant," or "We're relatively distinct, however connected"—can make the same antiparochical difference (Geertz 1983). Both are valuable intellectual and rhetorical resources; their critical complementarity is especially visible (segmentary politics-style) at the boundaries between anthropology and other disciplines.[8]

On the other hand, while objectivist and interpretive comparative analyses can be complementary, they also conflict—and strongly enough to have opposed perspectives on the criteria for the methodological and analytical adequacy constitutive of "proper" anthropology. The divergent stances may be uncompromisingly sharp. Two well-known examples are Marvin Harris's (1968) historically framed arguments for a materialist anthropology and David Schneider's (1984) culturalist critique of kinship constructs.

But more often than engaging one another, practitioners of each approach write as if the other does not exist. Take *Readings in Cross-Cultural Methodology* (Moore 1961), for example. This Human Relations Area Files volume aimed to collect "those papers of the past couple of decades generally deemed most significant, along with examples of earlier efforts," and it promised "to give a view of the development of cross-cultural comparative studies," presenting "the basic theoretical and methodological problems involved" (iii). But while the collection included Tylor's "On a Method of Investigating the Development of Institutions" (1888), it neglected to include Boas's "The Limitations of the Comparative Method" (1940a [1896]), without a word of explanation. In anthropology at large, mutual accusations of misrepresentation, or of leaving the fold intellectually and/or ethically, are muted by the rarity of regularized contexts for explicit engagement (Ingold 1996a ix, although Ingold (1996b) itself is a provocative exception).[9]

"Two Cultures" (after a Fashion) Everywhere

I have been using comparativism as a lens for viewing *intra*-sociocultural differences but could have illustrated the tension between positivist and interpretive approaches within this subfield using other literatures— "methods" discourse, for example. Bernard (1994) might be juxtaposed with, say, Marcus (1998, part 1): "two cultures" surely and each influential in the discipline. My larger point is, however, that rifts akin to this complex "two cultures" relation also occur within each of the other anthropological subfields (as well as outside these disciplinary spaces altogether— where others' invocations of anthropological knowledge require an effective response).

These kindred, internal rifts are suggested in the accounts of archaeology and anthropological linguistics elsewhere in this volume.[10] Within biological anthropology a related tension is evident, for example, in debates over "modern human" origins (Tattersall 1995; Thorne and Wolpoff 1981; Wolpoff 1980; see Peregrine, Ember, and Ember 2002 for several useful, accessible reviews and *Anthropology News* 44 (4) 2003, 25, for indications of how this debate is represented in popular media). Reflecting a profound philosophical/theoretical difference over the objective reality of "species" and the representation of evolutionary processes, one key argument within this debate has centered on how—or whether— to demarcate "modern humans" from "Neandertals." For example, in a recent talk at Princeton, Milford Wolpoff distinguished what he called "populationist" from "essentialist" approaches to the species question. In his view, the essentialist approach depends on defining a set of fundamental, invariant characteristics that all "modern humans" share (and non- "modern humans"—e.g., Neandertals—do not possess).[11] Wolpoff's populationist perspective, in contrast, emphasizes the wide range of physical characteristics of present-day peoples (all by definition understood to be "modern humans"). This approach construes human evolution as a gradual (and global) process involving distinguishable, but reproductively and socially interacting, regional populations. This makes reference to speciation an interpretive last resort since, Wolpoff noted, it makes little sense to search for the origin of "something" you cannot define.

Other examples could be cited.[12] My point here is *not* that populationist biological anthropologists have the same attitude to human variation as interpretive cultural anthropologists, nor that arguments over "essentialism" have (essentially) identical characteristics in biological and cultural anthropology, nor even that biological anthropologists are divided around these issues to the same degree (or in the same proportions) that cultural anthropologists are.[13] There is, rather, a *family resemblance* among the kinds of disconnection that we all know exist *among* the four anthropological subfields and those that I have been characterizing *within each* of them. Despite the parallels, we tend to identify whole subfields with essentializing positivism or contextualizing interpretation so that polarized references to "science"—reductively (or situationally) representing objectivism or positivism or reductionism (not all the same thing)—can come to stand for the subfield problem or vice versa. The subfields thus appear to conflict simply *as wholes* when the polarizing animus resides also within each.

This muddle might deserve attention if our dilemma were (only!) the reconciling of a historically contingent disciplinary organization with in-

evitable shifts in specialist interests that always affect departmental business and individual scholars' preferred research collaborations. Although
all that is hard enough, our dilemma is not only this disciplinary (or
interdisciplinary) practitioner's affair. It also derives from the power of
the "two cultures" as an interpretive frame of reference in American culture *at large*, where we are both ambiguously and ambivalently placed as
experts. This framework shapes how nonanthropologists interpret our
work and, most certainly, our disputes—whether among anthropologists
of various kinds; between anthropologists and other specialists; or between ourselves and journalists, other cultural mediators, and publics, all
with interests different from our own.

What is more, despite our internal specialist differences, this popular
framing collectivizes us, and in a particular way. The putative subject
matter of our unique expertise—"Man" (as Clifford has invoked it) or the
diversely-but-distinctively Human—remains such an enduringly popular
object of desire that it is hard to avoid. Properly disciplined and held in
its "savage slot" (Trouillot 1991), anthropology's comparative, first-hand
point of view is expected to offer answers to questions other scholars and
laypeople have about fundamental "human nature."

This popular expectation was painfully clear when the news media
picked up the anthropological controversy over journalist Patrick Tierney's *Darkness in El Dorado* (2000). Tierney accused Napoleon Chagnon
and those with whom he worked of abusive research practices and im-
pacts on Yanomami communities. Although Yanomami research had been
sharply controversial within the discipline internationally for decades
(Nugent 2001; Wolf 1994), the dispute that erupted over Tierney's claims
and their accuracy prompted investigations by several universities and
academic societies, notably the AAA. As an example, consider how the
New York Times represented the controversy in the first "Week in Review" section article to appear after initial news reporting about the im-
minent publication of Tierney's book (and its then upcoming excerpt in
The New Yorker):

> Anthropology is riven by two opposing worldviews. Sociobiologists,
> who believe that humans across the globe share an essential nature
> shaped by evolution, love [Napoleon] Chagnon's work. It confirms
> their suspicion that men from South America to Serbia are driven
> by aggression. Cultural anthropologists, who emphasize the impor-

tance of local context and recoil at universal statements about human behavior, think Mr. Chagnon's conclusions are pure fantasy.

Steven Pinker, a sociobiologist who teaches cognitive science at MIT, liberally cites Mr. Chagnon's work in his book *How the Mind Works.* "Chagnon is a great empiricist," he says. "Sadly, most anthropology is off the scale in post modernist lunacy. There's this orthodoxy that says human nature is a blank slate. For telling it like it is, he has become public enemy No. 1."

John Tooby, a colleague of Mr. Chagnon's, agrees. "Anthropologists are trained to appreciate cultural differences, but they can't stand it within their own profession," he says (Zalewski 2000, 2).[14]

In the passages above and elsewhere in the article, the author conjured up a series of intra-anthropological oppositions: "sociobiology" versus "cultural anthropology"; "empiricist" versus "post modernist"; "evidence" versus "ideology"; "universals" ("essential [human] nature," "evolution") versus "local context" ("human nature [as] blank slate"). The author identified "anthropologists" generally with the appreciation of cultural differences but asserted that "anthropology's original mission" has been "lost":

As [Paul] Rabinow puts it: "The idea of someone going to the most technologically simple societies and trying to learn lessons about human nature by studying them, that's been refuted."

To simply observe a threatened culture, as Mr. Chagnon did, is now considered irresponsible; the anthropologist needs to be first and foremost an activist. Indeed [Nancy] Scheper-Hughes says that anthropologists these days are more concerned with "critiquing globalization" than studying local traditions (ibid).

It might not be much of a stretch to read the article's reference to activism here as suggesting that many anthropologists have abdicated scholarship generally and science ("observation," studying "human nature") specifically. In this way, the article suggested that anthropologists have lost their professional way. The exhortation that they need to shape up, quit acting like the savages they study, and get back to writing about human unity-in-diversity was even more explicit in conservative media sources like *National Review.* But even the *New York Times* needed only a few paragraphs—aided by a bit of sensational/ironic color in the article's title ("Anthropology Enters the Age of Cannibalism") and language (labeling anthropological disputes "blood feuds" and "fratricide")—to identify anthropology with its "savage slot" both coming (its mode of impropriety) and going (its proper object). Proper anthropology was characterized by an older "faith" in the ability to "observe foreign cultures . . . and, in some deep way, understand them" in terms of "sweeping interpretations," Chagnon's work being the exemplar. At the same time, Chagnon's anthropology was labeled "sociobiology" (*not* "cultural anthropology") for facing the ugly possibility of an agonistic human nature.

My point is that, as in many other public contexts, in this case the four-subfield relationship was the least of our worries. Instead, for their readers, journalists translated a long-standing dispute among *sociocultural* anthropologists as a "two cultures" conflict between scientific (sociobiological, generalizing) researchers and their putatively antiscience (postmodern, activist) opponents. In this light, first, our anticipations of that popular interpretive framework may be more significant than our management of the four subfields as such. Second, the conflict carried with it contradictory assumptions about the value of science and its alternatives that we would be wise to recognize. Finally, reflected in our public's eyes, we are still all about foundational inquiry into the essence of "what it means to be human." Many of us may want to change this designation. We may or may not consider the matter a maddeningly redundant distraction. But so long as people—our interlocutors in classrooms and academic meetings, at home, in everyday life, and in our research settings—have this in mind, we will have to think through the implications of withdrawing from the conversation.

Considering how the four subfields have been practiced may develop these observations about how our work and disputes are translated for public consumption. In the next section, moving between disciplinary and personal history, I illustrate how the subfield "bundle" has not always been sacrosanct; it has also been deployed selectively in pursuit of particular questions. In the final section of this chapter, I suggest how a panoramic view of contemporary anthropological practice may reframe strategies for the future. Practitioners of the separate subfields have been concerned with how existing intradisciplinary relationships limit us, how they draw us away from the interdisciplinary connections we would prefer to elaborate. But we also face other powerful constraints. The furor provoked by Patrick Tierney's book is just a recent example of how public discourse draws us into inter- and extradisciplinary associations *not* of our choosing. What might it take to have an audible voice and a distinctive, not simply redundant, impact in those unchosen, undisciplined contexts? Answers might help us to imagine a disciplinary future premised neither on fission nor "holistic" fusion.

Cultivating Cross-Subfield Accents:
The Pragmatics of Subfield Relations

In the abstract, appeals to four-subfield "holism" have a ritualized ring, as anyone browsing anthropology department websites around the United States might notice. My own search of departmental mission statements posted on these sites yielded many very similar paragraphs rationalizing local four-subfield course coverage aimed at undergraduate students (and occasionally at graduate students as well). These statements appeared most genuine—least formulaic and routinized—at schools where they were addressed to students considering vocational majors like nursing or business. Not surprisingly, a historical framework may help us make sense of these postings.

Disciplinary Historical Perspective

George Stocking has suggested that periodic reassertions of cross-subfield unity were as much strategic moves as consecrating ones. He noted that while Boas, the unifier, himself expected the subfields to split apart, "centrifugal forces were resisted" institutionally over the twentieth century. They were resisted because of the "potency" of holism as a disciplinary ideal and because of a *recurrent* "pragmatic need to represent a unified 'anthropology' to the world outside the discipline" (Stocking 1988, 19; see Yanagisako, this volume, for a different commentary).[15]

The occasion for Stocking's paper was the American Council of Learned Societies' request for an account of the development of anthropology "in relation to professional organizations and learned societies" (Stocking 1988, 17). In this context, it makes sense that Stocking attended to the discipline's organizational reassertions of unity. But the point applies as well to the history of anthropology's substantive concerns. We can read those invocations of cross-subfield "holism" in present-day departmental mission statements as echoes of such a history of strategic common causes.

Arguably the most significant of these causes is the discipline's engagement with "race" matters, American anthropology's defining issue (Stocking 1968, xxii–xxiv and ff.; see, e.g., Goldschmidt 2000 for an insider's retrospective). While Stocking's continuing historical studies have established the point, several recent works by anthropologists and others renew and strengthen it both historically and in relation to contemporary frameworks (e.g., Baker 1998; Caspari 2003; Liss 1998; Mukhopadhyay and Moses 1997; Harrison 1998b; Susser and Patterson 2000; Vitalis 2002). They illustrate and dissect both the strengths and the weaknesses of our biocultural experiment in particular.

It is important to remember how critical (perhaps heterodox) work in physical anthropology helped to establish the value of the Boasian "culture" concept in the first place; that concept was then deployed in policy-oriented studies to undo reigning biological ideas about the immutability of racial types.[16] Thus, in the 1880s, Boas's Baffin Island fieldwork aimed to demonstrate the experiential, situational (rather than innate, essential) character of sensory thresholds. This study in Fechnerian psychophysics provided an empirical rationale for promoting cultural relativism as a compelling explanatory framework. At the turn of the twentieth century, eugenics was on the verge of becoming a dominant "progressive" response in the United States to popular concern over rising immigration (Menand 2001, 381–383). In this context, Boas's subsequent large-scale study for the U.S. Senate's Dillingham Commission—which used the "cephalic index" and other statistics to demonstrate the *malleability* of "racial" physiognomies in immigrants and their children—similarly pursued questions and used methods at the juncture of biological and cultural anthropologies with the intention of changing racist public policy (Menand 2001, 383–386; see also Liss 1998, 139).

Boas maintained a vigorous public (not just academic) presence until his death—including collaborations with W. E. B. Du Bois and other African American scholars and public figures (Baker 1998; Liss 1998; Vitalis 2002). Nevertheless, this work did not have a notable impact until World War II, when discrepancies between foreign and domestic policy became visible enough to help begin a shift in public racial sensibilities.

The reasons for this ineffectiveness are complex (e.g., Liss 1998); I consider only a corner of the picture. Boas's studies were precursors of what physical anthropologist Alan Goodman (2001) has called "radical bioculturalism" or, as Mukhopadhyay and Moses (1997) put it, "embedding biology in society and culture" as a "radically different paradigm" for thinking about the biology/culture relationship. Without doubt, biological anthropologists (and the rest of us) have compelling reasons to be critical of their subfield despite its important transformations since the 1960s (e.g., Calcagno 2003; Goodman 2001; Stocking 1968, 163). Nevertheless, critical work in biological and cultural anthropology has the *potential* to be mutually reinforcing. This potential is admittedly fragile. It is easily undermined and remains unrealized insofar as the complex, complementary message is split apart and thereby simplified in academic or public discourse. Indeed, the dual Boasian argument about the biological meaninglessness of "race" categories but the social reality of cultural constructs *was* disarticulated when this work was incorporated, via Gunnar Myrdal's *American Dilemma*, into the Supreme Court's 1954 *Brown vs. Board of Education* (Baker 1998, ch. 8). Both Lee Baker and Eugenia Shanklin (1998) attribute what Baker calls our persistent "color blind bind" to an analogous separation of the biological critique of "race" from ethnographic and sociolinguistic studies of the reality and power of racial constructs in popular discourse. That is, we dull a potentially sharp point by persistently segregating biological and cultural arguments.[17]

Personal History: Morningside Heights, 1970s

Anthropology's antiracist side attracted many students of my generation—attending college and university in the wake of the Civil Rights Movement and war in Southeast Asia—who were also drawn in by its relativizing exposé of familiar assumptions (apparently including its own). My own graduate school experience, while not typical, offers another view of the situatedness of subfield connections. For over twenty years I have worked in a small, coherent, mostly sociocultural department and fully appreciate the peacefulness this situation has engendered.[18] But I was trained at Columbia: four-field heartland and Boasian central place. The subfield bundle was indeed an unquestioned condition of graduate training during my cohort's pre-fieldwork period in the mid-1970s, when (no matter what our interests) all students were required to take two semesters of each subfield.

But quite a few of us did more than that. At that time, the dominant theoretical orientations in our community were Marxian, feminist, and structuralist (with all sorts of internal arguments over versions of each). In this intellectual context, the folks I knew used cross-subfield connections to pursue particular topics we cared about. Coming into anthropology when we did, racism was a sharp issue for many of us. Intellectual movement back and forth across the sociocultural/biological divide was integral to critiques of the so-called "scientific racism" of Arthur Jensen, whose 1969 *Harvard Educational Review* argument about the genetic component in "racial" IQ differences was intensively dissected. Our cross-subfield reading supported counterarguments about the cultural politics of difference.

Similarly, cross-subfield movement helped to develop and strengthen an emergent feminist perspective on "sex roles" in anthropology. The two volumes that established an "anthropology of women" (Rosaldo and Lamphere 1974 and Reiter 1975) included contributions from the four subfields. While the distribution was heavily weighted toward the sociocultural, the inclusiveness helped promote kindred innovations in all the specialties. In any event, earlier publication of the *Man the Hunter* symposium (itself a four-subfield collaboration) and social evolutionary works like *Men in Groups* had demanded a correspondingly broad-spectrum response (Lee and DeVore 1968; Tiger 1969).[19]

Prompted at least in part by the Vietnam conflict, anthropologists were drawn into arguments about the nature of warfare. In those contexts, cross-subfield knowledge was used critically against ahistorical ethological or social-evolutionary explanations in terms of innate male "aggression" (like Konrad Lorenz's *On Aggression*).[20]

Theory-driven and topical cross-subfield engagements in the 1970s encouraged wide-ranging movements across disciplinary boundaries as well. General interest in structuralism, prompted by translations into English of the works of Claude Lévi-Strauss, led some members of my graduate student cohort to Piaget and other psychological work, to Chomsky and other nonanthropological linguistics, to intellectual history, literary theory, and philosophy, and to political economy. Tracking another (not unrelated) trend of the time, friends in archaeology and cultural anthropology were reading Marx and Braudel together, arguing about what kinds of historiography might be adequate to the nondocumentary sources we variously faced. History department friends, looking to expand their sense of sources and theory, were active in those extracurricular reading groups too.

Thus, in this perhaps peculiarly 1970s New York realization, there was nothing particularly sacred about the way four-subfield engagements were practiced. Rather than being generic, routinized, or prescribed, our rationales for moving around and among the subfields were specific, improvised, and topic- or argument-driven.

In retrospect, it is also evident that some of this movement was motivated by what was then the rhetorically powerful figure of "human" distinctiveness: how humans are alike in our differences from ants, wolves, or primates. Students of structuralism, for example, had reasons to follow connections, on one hand, to linguistics and, on the other, to brain studies and primate studies, especially comparing field studies of social animal communication, experiments with primate language acquisition, and linguistic analyses of "distinctively human" language. A culturally and linguistically alert archaeology and biological anthropology—attentive to emergent human "species specificities" centering on "symbolization" (or "the imposition of arbitrary form" on the material world [Holloway 1969]— helped to set up questions cultural anthropologists cared about. That is, during the 1970s, many of the folks I knew were struggling to get a *nonreductive* fix on "human nature," explicitly to clear a space for an emergent concept of "culture." At the time, it seemed quite possible to do this in a manner compatible with the work of *both* symbols-and-meanings-inclined *and* science-identified anthropologists across the subfields (e.g., Geertz 1962 [1973], 1964; also cited in Holloway 1969).

From this vantage, the four-subfield and "two cultures" problems converge over what I would like to call "strong reductionism." Not all science is reductionist in this strong sense: the epistemologically ambitious stance that explanations for complex phenomena must, in the final analysis, refer to regularities in the behaviors of their simpler components. A qualified reductionism may be consistent with cross-subfield communication. But that is not the case with contemporary descendants of the strong reductionism of Vienna Circle philosophers and scientists who launched the "Unity of Science" movement (Holton 1993; Weinberg 1993; Wilson 1996; and see the next section below). The explicit goal of strong reductionism has been to subsume all knowledge to fundamental (physical) laws. Contemporary proponents like Steven Weinberg and E. O. Wilson are intolerant of notions of "emergent" phenomena, relations, or principles. But other scientists (including prominent evolutionary biologists like Ernst Mayr) take explicitly antireductionist positions.

Over the past generation, many cultural anthropologists (including some of us former Columbia types) have devoted considerable single-subfield energy to unmaking an older culture idea in favor of a concept of cultural practice as discursive, enacted, contested, historical, and unbounded. Participating in cross-disciplinary poststructural scholarship has enriched our understanding of the politics of interpretation and translation. In the course of these efforts, we have elaborated extra-anthropological reading and collegial connections. But because of my earlier experience, I am inclined to view these innovations as both consistent with and enabled by certain antireductive insights that span the anthropological subfields.

Cross-subfield "holism" has never been practiced widely in the work of individuals (Calcagno 2003); nor has the work of any one subfield ever been of *general* interest to practitioners in the other subfields. However, nowadays as in the past, all of us regularly find ourselves in arenas of partially overlapping concern. Here and there in these arenas, something like the Boasian four-subfield pragmatic is being reinvented (e.g., Rapp and Disotell 2003). As Michael Silverstein argues elsewhere in this collection, there has been a mutual assimilation of linguistic and cultural anthropological understandings (if not methods and technical vocabularies) over the past generation or so. Accounts, like Ian Hodder's, of the diversification of archaeology in relation to trends in sociocultural anthropology identify the partially convergent interests of these two subfields in material culture studies and historiography, as well as in several topical areas (e.g., Gillespie, Nichols, and Joyce 2003). With respect to cultural/linguistic and biological knowledges, the anthropology of science, medical anthropology, and studies of gender/sexuality constitute zones of convergence. I am particularly struck by the continued force of four-subfield collaboration in its classic locus—in critical work on the "race" concept—evident in a wide range of recent publications (some of which are cited above).[21]

Nevertheless, our intellectual climate and worldly circumstances have clearly changed over the past twenty-five years. What is different now, such that reference to the specificities of "human nature" in particular is no longer second nature—which is to say that it no longer makes sense to many of us the way it might have?

Answers may be found in the analysis of conditions that have renewed the "two cultures" rift between humanists and scientists—the so-called "science wars." The expansion and redirection of interdisciplinary science studies since the late 1970s themselves followed shifts in relations within and among the sciences, in research funding across the disciplines, and in the social position and internal structure of universities, colleges, and secondary schools—all obvious contexts for the polarization. These shifts are connected with other vantages opened up in the post–Cold War world, which we have begun to explore.

Given anthropology's own institutional vulnerability during this time, it is not surprising that the frayed condition of our own internal quilting of objectivist and interpretive stances should reflect the global situation. It is not surprising that these stances have appeared simply polarized within and between subfields, making their partial connections both less evident and more awkward.

In this context, questions about "fundamental human nature"—still often popularly identified with anthropology as a whole—have grown increasingly distasteful to many cultural anthropologists. These questions put us in a compromised position, a double bind, as was evident in the *New York Times* article on the controversy concerning Tierney's *Darkness in El Dorado*, discussed above (although of course journalists have their own double binds). Background premises of the questions we are asked demand half of our attention even as we attempt a meaningful response. Thus when Paul Rabinow is quoted as explaining that anthropologists have refuted the idea of going to "technologically simple societies" to learn "lessons about human nature," we mentally add (as Rabinow may also have done) that, of course, Yanomami are not simple, technologically or otherwise (what with guns, cameras, and fax machines, not to mention transnational rights advocacy organizations), and so on and on. However, backing up, qualifying, and deconstructing the journalist's questions are doomed efforts when one gets only a sound byte. Lee Baker's analysis of how Boasian research on "race" was only selectively "woven into the nation's fabric" builds a powerful scaffolding for this point.

I suspect that in the past, the questions that drew out cross-subfield affinities appeared to come more often than not from inside anthropology across the subfields. The questions were our own. But over the past twenty-five years the specialist work of many sociocultural anthropologists has inclined steeply toward historical and literary/cultural studies, just as many biological anthropologists have turned to molecular genetics. Given this divergence, the four-subfield configuration looks increasingly outdated, an unproductive entanglement inhibiting the interdisciplinary exploration that subfield practitioners respectively desire: molecular biology or literary theory, cognitive studies or social history.[22] Questions that might have motivated cross-subfield moves in the past now seem exogenous, not founded in the experience of overlapping intra-disciplinary projects.

Nevertheless, the questions are out there. So perhaps we need to consider how to participate in inter- and extradisciplinary relations we do not choose. Inadvertent or unwelcome cross-talk may have become more frequent and challenging over the past generation, as a function of both increasing scholarly specialization and the changing sociopolitical circumstances of our work and research lives. How have these unchosen conjunctures amplified or otherwise inflected the internal disciplinary arguments I have been discussing? Answers might prompt us to think through the politics and rhetoric of self-representation in a larger culture in which reference to "science" carries complexly valenced authority. As the merest hint of how present these involuntary contexts are in our collective experience nowadays, consider the following five "unchosen grounds" for intra- and extra-disciplinary engagement.

Joint Departments

The bifurcation of Stanford anthropology into anthropological "science" and "cultural/social" departments (see Durham 1998; Yanagisako 1998) has had a palpable effect on other departments. While most of the departmental websites I have examined have unremarkable statements of a generally four-field sort, some schools (like Northwestern; Earle 1999) were specifically motivated by Stanford's reorganization. A few—for example, Emory (Paul 1987) and New York University (Rapp and Disotell 2003)—have for some time been explicit about intradisciplinary experimentation, while others—notably Rice (Marcus 1992)—have been equally deliberate about extended experimentation at the border of anthropology and the humanities.

It would be interesting to find out just how many four-subfield anthropology departments exist compared with un-four ones overall. But it would also be interesting to set those figures alongside the number of departments with other kinds of hybridities: anthropology/sociology may be the most common, but alternatives also exist, like the University of Illinois at Chicago's Department of Anthropology, which offers a program in geography. How do different departmental configurations affect practitioners' work and sense of disciplinary agendas and identities? In particular, we might ask with respect to anthropology/sociology departments how critical interpretive anthropologists negotiate the positivist, quantitative bias of much sociology. What does the four-subfield history of anthropology look like from that point of view?

Anthropologists in New Terrains

As our research sites and topics have expanded—postsocialist transition in Eastern Europe, corporate downsizing on Wall Street, ecotourism in South America—we and our students have found ourselves in heavily disciplined terrain (that policing itself being a potential ethnographic object). Practitioners from a wide range of academic specialties—less likely cultural studies than economics, political science, or medicine—evaluate our funding proposals, conference participation, and the like (whereas they are less likely to be evaluated by us). This was always true (even for those of us whose careers began in regional studies seemingly dominated by anthropology). But I would guess that the unwelcome pressure to engage other disciplines has intensified.

In my experience, graduate students and younger scholars have had difficulty devising styles of communication adequate to these situations. They have often been defensive about anthropological research methods and insufficiently prepared to argue, as often they must, for the specific value of anthropological perspectives. It seems that the more they encounter these kinds of "interdisciplinary" articulations, the more they need a convincing position on what their own disciplined contribution will be.[23] How have the four subfields experienced these conjunctures? How do interpretive cultural anthropologists, in particular, negotiate the (social) science emphases they regularly encounter?

Incursions onto Our "Turf"

Just as we have expanded outward in various directions, so too have other fields. As Emily Martin (2000) has recently argued, powerful new biological specialties have emerged in the past decade or two. They are absorbing an expanding share of the available research funding. Fields like sociobiology are by now well established in topical domains with which anthropology is also identified. Proliferating successors to sociobiology in the neurosciences (e.g., evolutionary psychology and most recently "neuroeconomics")—what Martin calls "neuroreductionisms"—continue to make claims concerning "human nature" that discount the research and analysis that all varieties of antireductionist anthropology have done on human sociality, cultural process, and cultural diversity.

Martin has discussed a number of disturbing examples in detail; I will add a related one to underline their influence. E. O. Wilson established sociobiology as a field with ambitiously reductionist goals a quarter century ago (1975, ch. 27). His *Consilience: The Unity of Science* (1998) updates the polemic and has been picked up prominently in literary media like *The Atlantic*, which published sections of the book and interviewed Wilson at length. Because of Wilson's scientific credibility, the New York Academy of Sciences used *Consilience* as the focus of a conference held in 2000 (Damasio et al. 2001). This meeting was organized specifically to undo the divisive mean-spiritedness of a 1995 New York Academy of Sciences–sponsored conference, "The Flight from Science and Reason," organized by *Higher Superstition* authors Paul Gross and Norman Levitt (about which see Ross, Martin, and other contributors to Ross 1996).

While the tone of this second conference was more pacific, the effect was contradicted by both the strong reductionism of Wilson's own argument and the structure and substantive emphasis of the proceedings.[24] As in *Consilience*, in his conference talk Wilson decried the chaotic "fragmentation of learning" associated with "the humanities and more humanistic social sciences." In contrast, the natural sciences "have evolved on their own toward internal unification" through "reductionistic analysis" (a good thing here), such that everything from particle physics through genetics and cell biology to ecology and cognitive neuroscience is "interconnected . . . by cause-and-effect explanation" (Wilson 2001, 12–13). There is nothing "strategic" about this unifying program. In contrast to the situational, intra-anthropological affinities that I have discussed, Wilson understands the unification of science to be an inevitability corresponding with the nature of objective reality itself.

Wilson declared that "mind and culture" are "material entities and processes," no more complex or "emergent" than those of other biological systems that, after some effort, have now been "broken down." Wilson identified four "borderlands originating from biology" that extend the unifying domain of the natural science into the relative chaos of humanistic studies: cognitive neuroscience, human genetics, human sociobiology (a.k.a. evolutionary psychology, etc.), and environmental biology. Bridging their way back across the chasm from the social science/humanities side, according to Wilson, are the two "consilient disciplines" of cognitive psychology and biological anthropology.[25]

And what is the main object of this bridge building? The Holy Grail of a consilient, unified science is that perennial object of popular fascination: human nature (or, as Wilson [2001, 14–15] prefers, "the epigenetic rules" or "inherited regularities of mental development"). Wilson figured that major progress had been made in discovering the genetically determined perceptual biases governing a number of important human traits. Of these he singled out "color classification and vocabulary," "incest avoidance," "aesthetic judgment," and "habitat selection" for discussion.

Apparently oblivious to relevant twentieth-century anthropological research, however, Wilson's discussions were painful simplifications. On the "evolution of morality," for example, he claimed that there is an "innate procedure by which people avoid incest, called the Westermarck effect after Edward Westermarck, the Finnish anthropologist who discovered it a century ago," and which has subsequently been "well documented in anthropological studies." It involves sexual desensitization of "people who live in close domestic proximity during the first 30 months of life of either one" (2001, 15–16)—a ghoulish unearthing of a deservedly dead idea. Or consider the claim that "if given free choice" of homesites, people "want to be on a height looking down to and across open savanna-like terrain . . . the environment in which our species evolved over many years". In what I take as an ominous warning to both urbanites and forest people, he adds with a wink that these features are "understood intuitively by landscape architects and real estate entrepreneurs everywhere" (16).

Martin (2000, 575) argued in an analogous context that insofar as explanatory frameworks like Wilson's strong reductionism resonate with our collective public culture, they reproduce and certify tacit "pictures of the world" that need rather to be questioned and transformed. These frameworks are recognized as up-to-date, authoritative versions of an already familiar image of naturalized individual agents. Their castigation of fragmentation and their utopian vision of unity and clarity provide a seductive confirmation of many people's everyday experience of social disconnection. Alternative understandings are all the more difficult to discern. We need to shine a brighter light so that images of social identities and cultural differences remain visible in the picture. This may require that cultural anthropologists make strategic common cause across subfield or disciplinary borders that we would not otherwise think to cross, as Martin has sought to do with cognitive scientist John Searle.

Practicing outside the Academy

With transformations in the job market for anthropology Ph.D.s since the early 1980s, it has been true now for quite some time that there are more anthropologists working outside colleges and universities than inside them. The divergent ethical codes of their respective professional organizations make evident some of the differences in the work structures of academic and applied practitioners.

There is now an extensive literature on the realignments by means of which individuals have negotiated partial or more complete shifts into nonacademic identities and commitments. For example, over the past few years, the *Anthropology Newsletter* has published several playful, critical, and thoughtful articles painting contradictory pictures of how anthropological expertise is understood in nonacademic contexts. Some reported finding that the "savage slot" image makes anthropology a "hard sell" and suggested ways of changing popular perceptions, while others discovered that it is "good press" (Erikson 1999; Lindstrom and Stromberg 1999). Elsewhere, there are signs of a popular reassessment of our identity. For example, a long *New York Times* Circuits section article, "Coming of Age in Palo Alto" (Hafner 1999, G1, 8)—the Margaret Mead reference inviting several different readings—reports with apparent delight that anthropologists like Bonnie Nardi have left or expanded their assigned "slot" to good effect. These anthropologists are replacing an old style of consumer research (which involved "only . . . asking people") with a new, much-needed "observational" approach (using "ethnographic skills by interviewing, watching and videotaping consumers in their natural habitats"). In addition to occasional pieces like this one that feature anthropology itself, numerous by-the-by references to contemporary anthropological practice (e.g., Lewis 2001, 34) are so very unmarked as to suggest that a new public perception is being normalized *even as* the old one still makes headlines (as in the Tierney/Chagnon case).

In any case, practicing anthropology as an independent consultant or in forensic analysis, contract archaeology, business, government, health care, and education clearly involves accommodations to nonacademic styles of research, analysis, application, and communication. It involves negotiating the privatization and commodification of knowledge and, I suspect, the rhetorical power of (social) science models of knowledge production. How do the four subfields and their mutual borrowings fare as resources or disabilities in these contexts (e.g., Gillespie et al. 2003, 5)? How might the discipline as a whole take account of these trends?

Public Voices

Finally—and complexly related to the preceding topic—within academic anthropology there is a radical ambivalence over being heard publicly. This ambivalence—about the ethical/political implications of variously positioned expertise and other things—is painfully evident in the last couple of years of articles in the *Anthropology Newsletter* and a range of other sources (e.g., Brettell 1993).

But the jig's up. The distinction between "informant" and "colleague," which formerly sheltered us from this conundrum, has utterly dissolved with shifts in our topics, sites, and jobs (not to mention with changes in the geopolitical position of even our most classic interlocutors). We know all too well how little control any author has over his or her products. This is true even within the confines of a relatively circumscribed, more or less disciplined audience—that is, even within the *conventional* scenes of strictly academic boundary crossing and internal dissension. But if and when (we should be so lucky!) our products cross over to a larger, more diverse crowd, we face a confluence of interlocutors with diverse and mutually contradictory claims to intellectual and moral authority: Samoan "free love"? The ethnicity of Kennewick Man? Truth and justice in the Amazon? "Yali's question"? With whom and when is it right to argue? When do we pick up or put down our pens?

We have been answering these questions in various ways. The shape of these responses is discernible in Nancy Scheper-Hughes's sound byte in Zalewski's *New York Times* article discussed above: in the emphasis and theoretical framing of our scholarly work ("critiquing globalization") and in varieties of not strictly academic activism (some of which are reported in *Anthropology News* and several other publications). Recent answers have shifted our concepts of "proper" anthropology by opening up the available subject positions and practices—for example, identifying alternatives to conventional field locations and relationships (e.g., Marcus 1995, 1999b; Martin 1994; Rabinow 1996).

But a number of other obvious tasks are less well developed—for example, public policy initiatives (for which our professional organizations are important) and involvement with the media and in education. For example, in his analysis of the history of "Western Civ" courses and texts, Daniel Segal (2000) provides a very specific and significant (although underestimated) grounding for our understanding of how notions of a primordial humanity out-of-time is kept alive in our cultural imagination. In complementary arguments, Eugenia Shanklin (2000) and others (e.g., Mukhopadhyay and Moses 1997) have charted changes in anthropology textbooks as a window on how we may (or may not) be teaching about "race" nowadays. Over the past few years, sources like the *Chronicle of Higher Education* and *Anthropology News* have discussed anthropologists' and other scholars' involvement in K12 and nonformal education (e.g., Cantrell 2003). From these accounts, it appears that our efforts to expand the public reach of anthropological understanding have been uncoordinated and ineffective compared with other academic disciplines like history and certainly like the sciences (which have long involved themselves in designing primary and secondary school curricula and communicating systematically with journalists and policy makers and for which public outreach is mandated as a condition of large-scale funding).

Accenting Anthropology: Holism is Not the Point

What might it take to have a critical, audible voice in circumstances of inadvertent, involuntary inter- and extradisciplinarity? One sign of disciplinary health might be rhetorical success in resignifying "anthropological" arguments in these contexts. That is, it would be a good idea for anthropologists not to be surprised in public if our necessarily esoteric specialist interests get translated broadly in terms of themes significant to the nonspecialist translator. Instead, we might make it our business to discover what those significant themes are and explore modes of engaging them, using a variety of resources. Insofar as anthropologists acknowledge that there is nothing natural or fixed about disciplinary borders, these resources will include the continued development of other collaborations and their dialects. But I suspect that these resources will also include the situational cultivation of cross-subfield accents (a bit of code switching, a creole nuance).

"Holism" is not the point. Fusion or fission are not our only options. Over its history, "four-field anthropology" as a pragmatically institutionalized discipline has produced humanist/scientist hybrids of various sorts; it has been the ambivalent guardian less of a "sacred bundle" than of a rare nesting ground—a condition of possibility—harboring anti-essentializing evolutionists, hermeneutic realists, and other third kinds. Keeping that fragile but powerful possibility open need not entail or imply a naturalized, dehistoricized, or bounded concept of disciplinary cultures. Acknowledging disciplines to be contingent, shifting *constructs* neither obviates nor undermines them nor makes them unreal. It states a mundane historical fact and challenges us to define, to articulate, our *creative responsibilities.* The definition I prefer—to preserve the social space for reinventions of our distinctive hybridity—implies an "ethnographic" project: that is, a quotidian, familiarized, contextual, pragmatically enacted attention to intersecting differences in the interest of cultivating voices with the historical depth and resonance to carry effectively, whether we choose the arguments we join or they choose us. There should be space enough, institutionally, for various partially connected realizations of the discipline—if not in particular careers or academic departments, then elsewhere in our reimagined community—where the issues, including strategies concerning our public contributions, can be articulated and argued over, rethought, and engaged.

NOTES

This chapter was originally presented at the symposium entitled "Unwrapping the Sacred Bundle: Reconfiguring the Discipline of Anthropology," organized by Daniel Segal and Sylvia Yanagisako, at the AAA annual meeting in San Francisco, November 2000. Thanks to Dan and Sylvia for organizing the symposium and to Dan Bradburd, Fred Errington, Deborah Gewertz, the Duke University Press readers, and my Princeton colleagues for helpful comments on drafts of this paper, but particularly to Dan Segal, whose patiently collegial skepticism forced me to elaborate my comments on biological anthropology and to be clearer than I probably wanted to be. I accept blame for the remaining obscurity. The final version of this chapter was completed in 2003.

1. That is, while I think there is a significant contrast between the ways "big science" and other kinds of research communities have learned to engage with and represent themselves to the public, there may be less of a contrast epistemo-

logically. Strong disagreements, comparable to those in the social sciences, also exist among natural science subfields (e.g., between solid-state and high-energy physics research agendas or between molecular genetics and both field ecology and developmental cell biology).

2. See below, but it might be worth clarifying right away that I do not mean a simple science/humanities polarization. The rift that concerns me divides a family of reductionist approaches aimed at abstracting essential invariants from a family of contextualizing approaches aimed at understanding complexity and variation. This constitutive opposition can be found both within and between particular science or humanities fields (as suggested in note 2, above).

3. As I suggest in this chapter's second section below, analogous (not identical) analyses may be made of each of the other subfields, including biological anthropology. (Although my remarks pertain to U.S. experience, they may be relevant to other national anthropologies; see, e.g., James 2002).

4. R. H. Barnes in particular begins his chapter by declaring, "Anthropology is permanently in crisis about the comparative method" (1987, 119), and he emphasizes the kinds of polarization I describe below.

5. With regard to critical assessments of Snow, I appreciate Stefan Collini's judgment that while specialization is unavoidable, we need "the intellectual equivalent of bilingualism" so as "to contribute to a wider conversation" about matters of public importance (1993, lvii). However, as I am doubtful that full bilingualism is possible, my title suggests a less ambitious goal (while playing with the biocultural-linguistic connotations of "cultivation"). Debates published in Ingold (1996b) are helpful explorations of the relative values and meanings of "generalization," "translation," and other categories central to anthropological varieties of the "two cultures" relation. The debates enact its practical, nonbinary complexity. Several of the essays in Ortner (1999a) also acknowledge this complexity.

6. For example, Holy sees a paradigmatic choice between what he calls "positivistic" and "subjective" approaches—that is, between "whether description of particular societies is merely the means to generalization, or whether description itself is the key task" (1987b, 1). He asserts that the positivist approach sets description and generalization in a means/end relationship; dissolving this relationship means cutting the "functional link" between comparison and generalization. From Holy's standpoint, comparison appears to be all and only about making "generalizations"; if one rejects the positivist project, one's only alternative is "subjective" particularist "description." This is not how many interpretive anthropologists (myself included) view our choices.

7. They may also refer to themselves as "science" in the sense of systematic, empirical study (as the natural sciences often sort themselves as generalizing and particularizing). For two provocative contextualizations, see Lévi-Strauss (1966) and Wagner (1981).

8. Examples are everywhere. We could include Malinowski's arguments addressing psychology or economics or Boas's work on the psychology of race and IQ testing. We could cite Africanist lineage theory in relation to Western legal and

political theory, Clifford Geertz's "cultural systems" essays, Marshall Sahlins's critiques of sociobiology and neoclassical economics, Mary Douglas's engagement with economics and environmentalism, and Marilyn Strathern's analysis of British legal debates around reproductive technologies and of "audit" culture.

9. In anthropology, argument may *be* theory (as Ingold suggested), but direct disagreement is often circumscribed. Regional ("culture area") literatures may be the most likely public sites for an analysis of our overt disagreements about approaches and results (Lederman n.d.). Other obvious sites—grant, manuscripts, and tenure evaluations—are, because of their confidentiality, harder to study.

10. Hodder refers to the divergent interdisciplinary interests of archaeologists, some (like many cultural anthropologists) orienting themselves to history and others collaborating with geophysical scientists. This diversity has implications for intradisciplinary relations among anthropological subfields. Anthropological linguists likewise have divergent collaborations—for example, with literary scholars on one hand and cognitive scientists on the other. At the same time, Silverstein notes that the linguistic/cultural distinction has collapsed for many of us. In what follows, my emphasis on the cultural/biological subfield relation is meant to complement the foci of other chapters in this collection.

11. This approach is based on the idea of "punctuated equilibria" in evolutionary process (Eldredge and Gould 1972). That Gould's work also reflects a historical sensibility (whether it concerns nature or biological discourse) raises interesting questions that I have no space here to consider.

12. With respect to methods for interpreting fossil remains, I am intrigued by edgy disagreements between those anthropologists who labor to devise objective quantitative measures for sexing skeletons and those who emphasize that only hands-on experience can really teach a person whether an "orbital border" is "soft" or not. Who is doing "proper anthropology"? What constitutes "good science"?

13. For an interesting account of the historical fortunes of anti-essentialist physical anthropology, see Caspari 2003, who also conveys both the historical depth *and the fragility* of this stance in that subfield. The special issue of *American Anthropologist* of which Caspari's paper is a part (Calcagno 2003), which reinforces that sense of fragility, came out as this collection went to press and cannot be discussed in the critical depth its relevance deserves.

14. Many other reports appeared both in the national print media (major newspapers and news magazines like *Newsweek*, together with their websites) and electronically (e.g., *Salon, Slate*, academic websites like that of the University of Michigan anthropology department), authored by journalists and by anthropologists and other academics. I focus in detail only on this one because of the influence of the *New York Times* and because I judge it to be both relatively moderate and representative of several key themes. I do not discuss the ways in which the *Times* or other media represented the central ethical/political matters that concerned the anthropological community but focus on how the apparent academic positions were themselves represented in these sources (though the two are related).

15. It is clear that "holism" is still a potent ideal for many anthropologists, even

in the face of evidence of its practical scarcity (e.g., Calcagno 2003). In this chapter, I am arguing neither for "holism"—as either ideal or practice—nor even for Collini's "multilingualism" (1993), but for creative reinvents of anthropology's distinctively hybrid disciplinary contribution.

16. It is ironic that an early effect of the growing dominance of Darwinism in late-nineteenth-century biological discourse was to undermine antecedent ideas about the possibility of racial "improvement," derived from Lamarck, with ideas about immutable types (Menand 2001, 382). In its contemporary variants, Darwinism proposes no such thing (see Peregrine et al. 2002, especially the chapters by Marks, Tattersall, Frayer, and Brace).

17. Baker (1998, 180–182) makes clear that the contingent political value of assimilationist arguments made by the "Howard Circle" was a rationale for this separation (thus their rejection of Herskovitz's "African roots" work). In this context, the biological critique of race was stressed, but the associated point about the historical specificity and relativity of cultures was dropped. Baker has interesting things to say about present-day versions of this same separation and retention of the biological point over the cultural in conservative legal arguments declaring "race" a nonissue. Julie Liss's complementary argument (1998, 153–154) provides sharply ironic insights into the ineffectiveness of both Boas's and Du Bois's interventions.

18. From the department's founding in the early 1970s, its faculty included an archaeologist and a linguist (out of a spare handful of faculty members); archaeology was represented until around 1990. While biological anthropologist Alan Mann, long at the University of Pennsylvania, visited Princeton every spring for years to teach a popular lecture course on human evolution, he has now joined Princeton full time.

19. Feminist anthropology has continued to be relatively inclusive (e.g., DiLeonardo 1990). Its ongoing contributions to medical anthropology and science studies—two of the most prominent contemporary topical emphases within sociocultural anthropology located at a juncture articulating biological, linguistic, and cultural knowledges—can arguably be understood in this light (see, e.g., Ginsburg and Rapp 1995).

20. Present-day critiques—for example, Whitehead (2000; cf. Otterbein 1999)—continue to historicize the issue and set it in a global framework. Tierney's dispute with Chagnon is relevant and demonstrates the difficulty of shifting media and public perceptions. I hope that it is clear that in all of the topical contexts I have mentioned, cross-subfield (and corresponding interdisciplinary) alliances were made on *both* sides of the arguments. The larger point remains that the "two cultures" problem generating many of these controversies transects anthropology's subfields.

21. The current state of cross-subfield connections in the different "culture area" literatures is also worth exploring, especially in light of the recent rethinking of fieldwork and area-oriented research (Marcus 1995).

22. Of course, not only biological anthropologists, but also many sociocultural

anthropologists collaborate with biologists, and both archaeologists and sociocultural anthropologists consult historians.

23. For a thoughtful version of such a rubric, see New York University "Sociocultural Anthropology Mission Statement": www.nyu.edu/gsas/dept/anthro/gradcultling.html.

24. Although I will cite only the 2001 conference publication here, my comments are based on attending both conferences and speaking with a wide spectrum of the participants.

25. Indeed the siren song would be even stronger if biological anthropologists were trained, hired, and tenured mostly in biology departments, given the present cachet of molecular biology. This ought to be reason enough for reserving disciplinary space for biocultural scholarship within anthropology.

Flexible Disciplinarity
Beyond the Americanist Tradition

A pair of divergent narratives surfaces frequently in discussions among anthropologists about the four-field configuration of the discipline in the United States. The first, which I initially heard voiced by my professors in the four-field department where I was trained, is a nostalgic narrative that attributes the decline in dialogue among scholars in the four fields to their increasing "specialization." American anthropologists—it is claimed—were once broadly trained in all four fields and thus were able to integrate their work with that of scholars throughout the discipline. Underlying this lament is an implicit Durkheimian hypothesis that increasing specialization has undermined a former mechanical solidarity in which anthropologists engaged in similar, if not identical, forms of scholarly labor and thereby shared a common vision of the discipline. As this shattered mechanical solidarity has yet to be replaced by an emergent organic one, the presumption is that we live in a period of "lag," caught betwixt and between two modes of social solidarity. If we could only fully comprehend our distinctive roles in the collective anthropological project, an even stronger solidarity would emerge out of the functional complementarity of this new division of labor. Until then, it seems, we must vigilantly guard against the threat of "fragmentation" or, even worse, "balkanization," which is depicted as a nightmarish state of anarchic, internecine conflict.[1]

The second narrative is one I have encountered more often in conversations among colleagues who are less enamored of the four-field discipline. These colleagues are well aware that the debate over the four-field configuration is quintessentially American. Citing British and French anthropology as evidence of the viability of alternative disciplinary formations, they characterize American anthropology as a "historical accident"—the arbitrary outcome of a peculiar institutional arrangement lacking a coherent logic.

In this essay, I argue that both the narrative of increasing specialization and the narrative of historical accident obscure, at once, the ideological processes of settler colonialism that brought the four fields together in an uneasy alliance in the nineteenth century and the nationalist sentiments that maintained it in the twentieth century. The uneasy alliance—which was evident in the founding of the American Anthropological Association (AAA)—joined evolutionist approaches to human variation with historical approaches to cultural variation in the service of a "holistic" science of humankind. The forging of this awkward disciplinary project was anything but a historical accident. Rather, it was shaped by a national history of settler colonialism and its accompanying racializing processes of national identity formation.[2] At the center of these interlinked processes of national and disciplinary identity formation were Native Americans, who, until World War II, were the primary subjects of American anthropology. Unwrapping the sacred bundle reveals their languages, artifacts, bodies, and cultures alongside the four-field discipline and its evolutionist logic.

Attributing the current disengagement of the four fields to increasing specialization or to increasing temporal distance from the "historical accident" obscures the intellectual and political developments that have led to the unraveling of the nineteenth- and early-twentieth-century project of American anthropology, which was shaped by the settler-colonial project to both know Native Americans and confine them to a premodern past. While Native Americans provided the human subjects of American anthropology, classical evolutionism supplied the logic for joining together "the four previously disparate enterprises of ethnology, archaeology, linguistics and physical anthropology" in support of the progressivist vision of human macro-history that was the dominant ideology of England and the United States in the late nineteenth century (Adams 1998, 62). It is no historical accident that as progressivism declined in the twentieth century, the only place where this "rather odd and uncomfortable confederation of older parts lasted" (Adams 1998, 62) was in North America, where the connection among the four fields was "part of the total effort to define the American Indian in relation to the known worlds of nature and culture; something that became an overriding concern for Western thinkers from the moment when the New World was discovered" (Adams 1998, 255).

This awkward disciplinary alliance has been rendered less viable by the global political and economic transformations since World War II, which have altered the communities and locales that we study, the theories and methods we use to study them, and the relations between us and those we study. Sociocultural anthropologists, in particular, have grown increasingly critical of the racial and cultural hierarchies and political inequalities that are naturalized by evolutionist approaches to human diversity. This is not to say that sociocultural anthropologists reject Darwinian theories of human evolution, but rather that we reject explanations of human cultural and social variation that rest on untenable assumptions of "classical evolutionism" (Stocking 1987, 170). While a few ideas of "classical evolutionism," such as the belief in a single psychic nature of humankind, continue to be accepted by some scholars in all fields of anthropology, most have been firmly rejected.[3] Among these are the discredited notions that "certain contemporary societies approximate earlier stages of human development, that in the absence of historical data these stages may be reconstructed by a comparison of contemporary groups; and that the results of this comparative method can be confirmed by 'survivals' in more advanced societies of the forms characteristic of lower stages" (Stocking 1987, 170).

The rejection of social evolutionism by sociocultural and linguistic anthropologists has widened the schism between the former and the biological anthropologists and archaeologists who employ evolutionist approaches to explain human diversity, both biological and cultural. There are, of course, notable exceptions to the way scholars in the four fields align themselves in this disagreement, and I do not mean to oversimplify the schism (see Lederman, this volume, for a discussion of the "two cultures" of comparison in all fields of the discipline). Postprocessual archaeologists, for example, employ theories of meaning and social action that place them closer to sociocultural anthropologists than to processual archaeologists (see Hodder this volume). It seems futile, however, to deny that this disagreement has been central to the tensions and conflicts among the four fields and a crucial force for their increasing disarticulation in the United States.

These tensions and disagreements are hardly new; as we shall see below, they have been with us since the formation of the discipline. Nor has the ambivalent, vexed relationship between evolutionism and ethnology been limited to the United States. The institutional bundling of the two in a single discipline devoted to the holistic study of humankind, however, was forged within a particular history of nation formation in this country. A detailed tracing of the specific historical linkages between U.S. national identity formation and anthropological disciplinary formation is beyond the scope of this chapter. My more limited objective in the first section below is to show that the four-field configuration of American anthropology and the evolutionist logic binding it together are legacies of the settler-colonial nationalism that made Native Americans its significant "other." In the second section, I turn to a key moment in our history of disciplinary formation—the founding of the AAA—to show that deep disagreements over this configuration preceded the supposed "fragmentation" of the discipline.

Settler-Colonial Nationalism and the "Vanishing Native"

Hodder (this volume) notes that the involvement of British and European archaeology in the project of the nation-state—that is, in defining its antiquity and historical depth—led to its close alignment with the discipline of history.[4] In the United States, on the other hand, colonialism and empire have been viewed as more significant influences on the development of archaeology, which was focused on the project of knowing the Native American "other" (Trigger 1984). In this section, I suggest that the bundling of archaeology, ethnology, linguistics, and physical anthropology in the discipline of anthropology in the United States (and more broadly North America) was motivated by both the project of knowing the Native American "other" and the project of defining the nation-state. Indeed, these two projects were closely interlinked. As in Britain and Europe, archaeology in the United States was engaged in establishing the historical depth of the nation. In the United States, however, historical depth was established not by excavating the presumed biological ancestors of the citizens of the nation-state but by excavating their spiritual and evolutionary ancestors—namely, Native Americans.

Until World War II the primary subjects of anthropological inquiry in the United States were Native Americans (Adams 1998; Borofsky 2002; Bourguignon 1996; Darnell 2001; Patterson 2001; Stocking 1979), and few would dispute that this was crucial in the formation of the four-field discipline. In his analysis of the philosophical roots of American anthropology, Adams states the following:

I have long been convinced that the unifying cement of American anthropology, which brings a certain coherence to all its disparate parts, is not any particular body of theory or practice, but simply the "possession" of the American Indian as its main field of study. Among other things it continues to justify the four-field conjunction of ethnology, linguistics, archaeology, and physical anthropology—an unstable confederation that was brought together in the early days of anthropology, but that long ago came apart everywhere outside North America (1998, 6).

Bourguignon concurs that the four fields were brought together to answer questions "about the origins and true nature of Native Americans" (1996, 7).

It is less clearly accepted, however, that the drive to know the Native American was conditioned by a settler-colonial nationalism in which Native Americans served as "raw materials for the construction of settler-colonial claims of proprietorship over colonized territory" (Ben-zvi 2003a, 206). Anthropological interest in the "Other" was conditioned in the United States by a form of colonialism that differed from the overseas colonialism that shaped British and European anthropology.[5] Like overseas colonialism, settler colonialism in the United States generated powerful ideological processes that motivated and shaped the production of knowledge—both bureaucratic and academic—about "native others." In contrast to overseas colonialism, however, the physical and moral presence of the "native others" in the territory of the settler-colonial nation itself challenged settlers' claims to the land and their national identity. Settler-colonial anxieties about reproducing the "civilized" society of the colonial metropole have commonly led to the destruction or marginalization of indigenous peoples to clear the way for the transplantation of "civilization" (Fieldhouse 1982; Frederickson 1988). At the same time, the shallowness of native-born settlers' history on the land in comparison to that of indigenous peoples undermines the former's birthright claim to the national territory. These challenges to the legitimacy of settlers' claims encourage the formulation of "foundational claims" by settlers to establish their inalienable rights of proprietorship over settled space (Stasiulis and Yuval-Davis 1995). These foundational claims can take a variety of forms, including claims of knowledge about the national territory, its history, and its inhabitants. To "know" Native Americans and their history can be viewed as a form of establishing and legitimizing native-born settlers' claims of succession to that legacy and their deep historical roots in the land.

In spite of the critical reexamination in the last four decades of the relation between anthropology and colonialism (Asad 1973; Fabian 1983; Kuper 1988), the crucial role of settler colonialism in shaping anthropology in the United States—and more broadly North America—has yet to be adequately scrutinized.[6] This can be attributed in part to a nationalist rhetoric and historiography that have obscured the colonization of Native American peoples and lands by restricting the "colonial period" to the period of British control prior to the American Revolution (Ben-zvi 2003a, 6). It is also due in part to the effective erasure and marginalization of Native Americans as coeval members of contemporary American society. This erasure and marginalization was facilitated by some of the very forms of knowledge production through which scholars and laypeople attempted to "know" them.

This complex mix of knowledge production and erasure of indigenous peoples is strikingly displayed in the work of Lewis Henry Morgan. Morgan's ethnological research on the *League of the Ho-de'-no-sau-nee, or Iroquois* (1954), his comparative study of kinship in *Systems of Consanguinity and Affinity of the Human Family* (1870), and his progressivist model of human cultural evolution in *Ancient Society* (1985 [1877]) have long been recognized as pioneering and crucial in the formation of anthropology in the nineteenth century.[7] Less widely recognized is the way in which Morgan's scholarly project grew out of his desire to forge a distinctive American national identity and destiny by drawing on the history and experiences of Native Americans. Prior to initiating his ethnological investigations of the Iroquois, Morgan had formed with friends a literary fraternity called the Gordian Knot, which looked to both Greco-Roman classicism and Native American myths and histories for inspiration in developing a national literature (Deloria 1998, 73). Morgan and his friends celebrated the noble savagery of the Iroquois, at the same time lamenting the loss of their poetic eloquence. In their "Indianization" ceremony, they assigned themselves Indian names and donned Indian costumes, transforming themselves into the spiritual descendants of the Iroquois.[8] Their project appears to have been incited by deep settler-colonial insecurities—

not unusual among well-educated, upper-middle-class Anglo-Americans in the nineteenth century—about the literary and, more broadly, cultural production of the United States in comparison to the metropole of Europe.

This romantic quest for literary inspiration soon evolved into a quest for empirical knowledge, as Morgan and his friends sought more detailed, accurate accounts of the Iroquois confederacy upon which they hoped to model the constitution of their club (Trautmann 1987: 10):

> Beginning with romantic notions of vanishing Indians, Morgan's New Confederacy (or Grand Order) of the Iroquois eventually turned from nostalgia toward rationalized, objective scientific investigation. Fictional creation gave way to the compiling of factual knowledge, and what had begun as an effort—firmly rooted in the consciousness of the Revolution and the early Republic—to define a literary national identity took on a modern, ethnographic character well suited to the American social elite of the late nineteenth century (Deloria 1998, 73).

Studying the history of the Indian and recovering his footsteps became a duty for Morgan, because "this race must ever figure on the opening page of our territorial history" (Morgan 1851, 60). This was especially the case as "nothing that may properly be called the Iroquois can now be found among us. Their Indian empire has passed away without leaving a vestige or memorial" (Morgan quoted in Deloria 1998, 77).

Morgan's mapping of the "disappearing" culture of the Iroquois was steeped in progressivist ideas of cultural evolution. In *Ancient Society*, Native Americans become the cultural ancestors of European Americans by way of the ancient Greeks and Romans. In his evolutionary narrative, the Native Americans who have been "left behind" in the stage of barbarism function as "our ancestors." For Morgan, the "career" of mankind had but one origin and one "uniform channel" on all continents. Thus, "It follows that the history and experience of the American Indian tribes represent, more or less nearly, the history and experience of our remote ancestors when in corresponding conditions" (Morgan 1877, xxxi). In addition, by drawing on accurate, empirical knowledge of Iroquois political and social organization, Morgan hoped to develop a more advanced model of democracy that would propel the United States beyond Europe and its class-encumbered society. Although they were frozen in the stage of barbarism, the Iroquois provided a model for American democratic society because their confederacy was the birthplace of the "principle of democracy" (Morgan 1851, 73).

Morgan's treatment of Native Americans illustrates what Fabian (1983) has called "allochronism," the discursive practices through which anthropologists deny that they and their subjects coexist in the same time period. Although ethnographic knowledge is produced through intersubjective communication between anthropologists and their subjects, this intersubjectivity has generally been suppressed by the distancing discourse of ethnographic representations, which relegates subjects to earlier stages of cultural evolutionary development (e.g., "savagery" and "barbarism"). Forged at the historical conjuncture of European colonialism and the decline in the authority of a biblical temporal narrative, anthropology reworked Enlightenment progressivist beliefs into scientific discourse through cultural evolutionary models such as Morgan's. The "denial of coevalness" between anthropologists and "Others" (Fabian 1983) is not limited to American anthropology; it pervades Anglo-American and French anthropology as well. In the United States, however, the suppression of the coevalness of Native Americans and anthropologists was shaped by a settler-colonial nationalism that simultaneously excluded Native Americans from the modern nation-state and defined them as our remote ancestors.

The anthropological fascination with Native Americans has been neither simple nor consistent. It has been ambivalent, heterogeneous, contradictory, and changing, ranging from evolutionist-progressivist models such as Morgan's to bureaucratic-administrative projects aimed at "uplifting" and integrating "our natives" into modern American society to ethical-retributive efforts aimed at "salvaging" their cultural traditions and advocating their self-determination. As we shall see below, these ethical-retributive commitments—which were already present in Morgan's work and actions—have become increasingly dominant in the "Americanist" focus on Native Americans since World War II. Already by the late nineteenth century, in the period preceding the institutionalization of anthropology in universities, the more violent era of extermination and displacement of Native Americans had been succeeded by an era of bureaucratic governance that including mapping, collecting, and curating knowledge of Native Americans and their past. The project to know the Native American, which Adams has labeled "Indianology," attained its greatest professionalization in natural history museums and the Bureau of American Ethnology (Adams 1998; Bernstein 2002; Hinsley 1992). Much of this work was undertaken by self-trained anthropologists who were wedded to an evolutionist paradigm (Hinsley 1992).

By the end of the nineteenth century, a new challenge to the way in which Native Americans were to be known was posed by the first cohort of academic anthropologists. This rising group of newcomers, who were led by Franz Boas, came predominantly from the German or German-Jewish intellectual community in and around New York City (Bunzl 1996; Stocking 1974; Adams 1998). They advocated a relativistic, nonevolutionary approach to studying the "historical differentiation of human groups" (Stocking 1988, 19).[9] Boas's relativist critique of evolutionism signaled the shift from "classical" evolutionary anthropology to the modern anthropological concept of culture (Stocking 1979, 9).

Wrapping the Sacred Bundle: The Founding of the AAA

In an article entitled "Guardians of the Sacred Bundle: The American Anthropological Association and the Representation of Holistic Anthropology," George Stocking (1988) notes that before the founding of the AAA in 1902, there were three institutional centers of anthropology in the United States.[10] These included (1) in Washington, D.C., "a well-established corps of government anthropologists, employed by the Bureau of American Ethnology and the United States National Museum of the Smithsonian Institution, who were on the whole strongly committed to social evolutionism";[11] (2) in Cambridge, Massachusetts, "a smaller group of somewhat less doctrinaire archaeologically oriented anthropologists at the Peabody Museum" at Harvard; and (3) in New York, under Boas's leadership, "a group of anthropologists at Columbia University and the American Museum of Natural History, who were critical of evolutionism, and who were associated with the American Ethnological Society, a preevolutionary anthropological group gone moribund in the 1860s which had been revived by Boas in the late 1890s" (Stocking 1988, 17–18).

Stocking recounts how in the fall of 1901, Boas and W. J. McGee, the acting chief of the Bureau of American Ethnology, began to explore the possibility of a national organization. A clear difference in the perspectives of these two men surfaced in the course of their discussions. McGee, described by Stocking as "a frontiersman with no academic connection who had moved easily from amateur natural history to semi-professional geologizing before sliding across into anthropology," favored an "inclusive" membership policy that would encourage the growth of local anthropological societies. Boas, "who was engaged in building an academic anthropology that would provide a rigor analogous to that of his own academic training in physics, favored an 'exclusive' principle" (1988, 18). As a result of McGee's political maneuvering and "double dealing," which Stocking (1960) documents extensively, the AAA was incorporated as an inclusive organization. Stocking concludes that "McGee won the battle, insofar as the AAA was founded in 'inclusive' terms, but Boas won the war," mainly because Boas produced "new anthropologists in his own image," while the evolutionists "left no academic progeny of their own" (1988, 18).

A second dimension to the disagreement between Boas and McGee over the inclusiveness of the AAA is even more relevant to anthropology today. This was the question of the inclusion of the four fields and the unity of the discipline. A couple of years after the founding of the AAA, Boas defined the "domain of anthropological knowledge" as consisting of all four subdisciplines, which he viewed as "unified by an underlying historical perspective" and as providing "evidence of the recent historical differentiation of human groups." McGee and other evolutionists, on the other hand, "assumed (on the basis of methodological assumptions that Boas criticized) that each of these four inquiries provided evidence of the generalized development of humankind from a mute and cultureless primate form." For Boas, however, "the unity of the inquiries that contributed to anthropology was an historically contingent phenomenon" (Stocking 1988, 19). Thus, he wrote in 1904:

> The field of research that has been left for anthropology in the narrower sense of the term is, even as it is, almost too wide, and there are indications of its breaking up. The biological, linguistic, and ethnologic-archaeological methods are so distinct that on the whole the same man will not be equally proficient in all of them. The time is rapidly drawing near when the biological branch of anthropology will be finally separated from the rest, and become part of biology. This seems necessary, since all the problems related to the effect of geographical and social environment and those relating to heredity are primarily of biological character. Problems may be set by the general anthropologist. They will be solved by the biologist.

Almost equally cogent are the reasons that urge on to a separation of the purely linguistic work from the ethnological work. I think the time is not far distant when anthropology pure and simple will deal with the customs and beliefs of the less civilized peoples only (Boas 1904, 35).

The disagreements over "inclusion" in the formation of the AAA encapsulate the ambivalent and tenuous alliance forged between Boas's project of drawing on the four fields to marshal evidence of the recent differentiation of peoples and McGee's project of encompassing variations in culture, language, and biology in an evolutionary framework.

The forging of the four-field discipline, of course, was not a one-time-and-forever event. As Clifford (this volume) points out, the articulation of the four fields in American anthropology, like all articulations, has had to be made and remade through historically contingent actions. Hence, while it was initially forged in the late nineteenth century, it has been remade in a number of different political-cultural-academic contexts. During the interwar years, for example, the four-field configuration was continually challenged by centrifugal tendencies as separate professional associations were formed in physical anthropology, linguistics, and anthropological archaeology (Stocking 1988, 20). Yet a semblance of institutional unity was sustained at several critical moments when these centrifugal forces threatened to divide the discipline. According to Stocking, "That these centrifugal forces were resisted has been due in part to the potency of a normative image of a 'holistic' anthropology that has been infrequently and imperfectly realized in actual disciplinary practice, and in part to the pragmatic need to represent a unified 'anthropology' to the world outside the discipline" (1988, 19).

Stocking concludes that during the post–World War II era, it was the predominantly pragmatic concerns of a growing number of professional anthropologists that held sway when the unity of the discipline was challenged. In the immediate postwar years, these professional anthropologists—half of whom were engaged in some kind of war work—argued for a vision of the "essential core" of anthropology as the "comparative study of human biology, language and culture." They did so primarily on the grounds that an inclusive discipline that claimed "for itself the status of a 'science' would be more effective than a congeries of independent sub-disciplines in representing the needs of professional anthropologists in the brave new postwar world of governmentally subsidized science" (Stocking 1988, 21). In the early 1980s, it was a challenge from an Internal Revenue Service audit calling into question the AAA's tax-exempt status that precipitated a reorganization of the association and, for the first time, the inclusion in the articles of incorporation of a statement defining the association's purpose as the advancement of "anthropology as the science of humankind in all its aspects, through archaeological, biological, ethnological and linguistic research" (Stocking 1988, 22–23).

The "pragmatic concerns"—or, more accurately, the ideological production of discourse about the "pragmatic concerns" of anthropologists—undoubtedly have been a crucial force in the reproduction of the four-field discipline. The "normative image of a holistic anthropology," I suggest, has been at least an equally powerful force of reproduction. This normative image has been fueled by complex sentiments and commitments that have been forged at, and have transformed with, specific political-cultural-academic conjunctures. In the 1950s and 1960s, for example, anthropologists' commitment to racial equality and the Civil Rights Movement gave physical anthropology and sociocultural anthropology a common cause (see Lederman this volume). Indeed, as a recent special issue on race of the *American Anthropologist* (1998, 100[3]) demonstrates, the struggle against racism and racial hierarchies continues to be a key motive for maintaining the collaboration between sociocultural and physical anthropology. The resurgence of evolutionary approaches to culture—as, for example, in the neoevolutionism of Leslie White (1959), Marvin Harris (1968), and others—has also engendered support for the four-field discipline.

Reconfigured settler-colonial nationalist sentiments provide yet another motive. The ardent defense of the four-field discipline is commonly infused with nationalist or regionalist (U.S. and Canadian) sentiments of loyalty to what is viewed as a distinctive American anthropological tradition. Some American anthropologists seem driven by a "disciplinary patriotism" to secure for perpetuity the sacred trust of their predecessors: the holistic four-field bundle and the knowledge of the history and culture of Native Americans. As Adams notes, "long after evolutionism waned [and] the four field schema lost its basic rationale," anthropology in the United States continued to be fueled by powerful sentiments of attachment to Native Americans (1998, 369). The drive to know the Native American is, for Adams, an "intellectual and moral passion" that "remains an important feature of the general American ethos, but more specifically of the ethos of American anthropology": "I think it is safe to say that a great many American anthropologists, including many who have never worked among the Indians, nevertheless retain a kind of proprietary/paternalist attitude toward them" (1998, 194).

Even with his acute awareness of the proprietary/paternalistic attitudes accompanying this interest in Native Americans, Adams remains committed to "Indianology": "an American anthropologist—whatever his or her special interests—who does not know the basic American Indian ethnographic data is like a professor of English who has not read Shakespeare. It is not a question of speciality; it is a question of basics. Not to know the Indian data is not to know why we are who we are" (1998, 6).

Furthermore, "the Indian is uniquely 'ours,' along with the grizzly bear and the Grand Canyon and the Rocky Mountains. He helps define what America is because he is something we don't have to share with Old World nations, who can only enjoy and appreciate and study him at a distance" (194). Indeed, for Adams, the physical propinquity to Native Americans and their "sense of a shared identity and shared experience" have led American anthropologists to "feel closer to their subjects, and to identify with them more than have other anthropologists" (256). In contrast to the "denial of coevalness" of anthropologist and native in earlier ethnographic representations, here the copresence of both in the same national space transforms the radically different experiences of predominantly white anthropologists and Native American subjects into a "shared experience."

Darnell similarly makes no excuses for undertaking a presentist history of the discipline in the name of reconstructing the "Americanist" tradition of our "elders," which she views as "the fundamental character of North American anthropology" (2001, xvii). The Americanist tradition, for Darnell, developed around the wide-ranging study of the American Indian and is associated with the historical particularism of Boas and his students. Although she views this tradition as having been eclipsed in recent disciplinary memory, it operates for her as an unseen national ethos that ultimately differentiates American anthropologists from others:

> I am increasingly convinced that there is a deep and long-established gulf across national traditions. American, British and French anthropologists, for example, far too often talk past one another without realizing they do so (2001, 21).

Anthropologists trained in North America since the Second World War, which includes most of our living elders, have absorbed the basic tenets of the Americanist tradition almost subliminally, without necessarily thinking of themselves as Americanists. . . . So the substratum of unquestioned Americanist assumptions became more and more deeply masked from conscious awareness (2001, 27).

Darnell's vision of the "Americanist tradition"—which is at once both historical and essentialist—entails an impassioned attachment not only to Native Americans as ethnological subjects, but also to the corpus of texts and records on them collected by American anthropologists. Her account of Sapir's reaction to Radcliffe-Brown's dismissive attitude toward the Native American language texts that Sapir and others had collected demonstrates that for her the record of the Native American past remains a crucial component of the sacred bundle. When Sapir resigned from the University of Chicago to move to Yale's Institute of Human Relations in 1931, he left behind a well-funded research program and field school with the Navajo. Sapir assumed that the chairman of the Chicago anthropology department, Fay-Cooper Cole, who was also a former Boas student, would look after the publication of the Navajo texts that had been collected under Sapir's auspices by Father Bernard Haile and his native "informant." Radcliffe-Brown, who had recently arrived at Chicago, however, expressed some doubt as to "just what one does with such texts." According to Darnell, "Sapir recoiled at this challenge to the very premises of the Americanist method and the almost sacred integrity of the texts," describing Haile's texts as "a priceless linguistic document" (Sapir to Cole, May 22, 1932; quoted in Darnell 2001, 22). In a later letter to Cole, Sapir characterized Radcliffe-Brown's disregard for the texts as follows: "It was all very much as though some Smart Aleck were to put the proffered texts of the Homeric poems aside with a supercilious remark about how much more interesting it would be if the author of these useless poems could only be persuaded to prepare a monograph on the Greek mystery cults for us" (June 2, 1932, University of Chicago anthropology department documents; cited by Darnell 2001, 22; see also Stocking 1979, 20).

Sapir was in good part reacting to the ahistorical scientism of Radcliffe-Brown's synchronic, functionalist approach to culture and society, which contrast dramatically with his humanistic search for meaning (Stocking

1979, 21). At the same time, however, Sapir's comparison of Navajo texts to the Greek "classics," which the British viewed as their ancient cultural legacy, leaves little doubt that for Sapir, as for a good many U.S. anthropologists (including Darnell), Native American texts and traditions constitute our distinctive national legacy. Unlike Morgan, Sapir did not view Native Americans as the evolutionary ancestors or even the spiritual ancestors of contemporary European Americans. That aspect of the Americanist tradition appears to have died out, for the most part, by the end of the nineteenth century. In contesting Radcliffe-Brown's implied distinction between a valorized high culture of "European tradition" and a marginalized ethnographic tradition of Native Americans, Sapir reaffirmed a central commitment of the Americanist tradition—the duty to honor and protect Native American culture for posterity.

Beyond Americanist Anthropology

The uneasy alliance between Boas's historical project and McGee's evolutionist project may have made sense at the beginning of the twentieth century, when a progressivist model of evolutionary development dominated academic and public understandings of human diversity. The newly constituted discipline of anthropology provided a strategic terrain on which to challenge progressivist ideologies of race, culture, and society.[12] Over the past century, especially since the civil rights era of the 1950s and 1960s, progressivist ideologies have waned both inside and outside the academy. This is not to say that such discourses do not resurface time and again—as, for example, in the debate over *The Bell Curve* (Hernstein and Murray 1994) in the 1990s—or that there is no longer a need for anthropologists to lend their expertise to antiracist projects. Biological essentialist schemes of racial hierarchy, however, are only one of many forms racism can take. The emergence of other forms of racial discourse and inequalities calls for different conceptual and methodological tools than those produced by the collaboration between sociocultural and biological anthropologists. In recent years, new conceptual approaches to the discursive and institutional production of historically specific forms of racism have proven especially useful in helping us analyze culture itself as a site of political struggle (Gilroy 1990, 1991, 2000; Goldberg 1990, 1993, 1997, 2002; Moore, Kosek, and Pandian 2003). Gramscian political theory, for example, has been more productive in understanding the naturalizing power of racial discourses than marshaling the four fields to speak with a "unified voice."

International political and economic developments since World War II have drawn the focus of U.S. anthropologists away from Native Americans to other peoples, other sites, and other issues, including other insecurities. Overseas research under the aegis of "area studies" was construed to be in the national interest and supported by government funding. Since the late 1960s, increased Native American political activism and agency has restricted the access of non–Native American anthropologists to Native American communities. Since then, most of the research on Native Americans has been done by archaeologists and linguistic anthropologists. Research on the social and cultural dynamics of contemporary Native American communities has shifted to scholars of Native American studies. At the same time, critical theories of nationalism have led sociocultural anthropologists to distance themselves from nationalist projects, including racializing processes of national identity formation, and to instead engage in critical analysis of them. The conceptual tools that have been most productive in understanding these processes and related cultural politics of gender, class, ethnicity, transnationalism, and globalization have come from outside the discipline—from feminist scholarship, critical race theory, literary analysis, and discourse analysis. Evolutionary approaches to race, despite having been reenergized by advances in molecular biology, have been of little use in understanding the social and political dynamics of race.[13]

The skepticism that Boas expressed at the beginning of the twentieth century about the comparativist search for the universal laws of culture, moreover, has multiplied in the face of the increased interconnections among the "human groups" we study. Treating these groups as discrete social units has become increasingly indefensible, as have the forms of comparative analysis than hinge on this assumption. Ethnographic and historical analyses that track the material and cultural flows across the presumed boundaries of social fields have flourished in cultural and linguistic anthropology. Evolutionary approaches to cultural diversity have little, if anything, to offer this project. Indeed, critical cultural theories of race, nation, gender, and class offer trenchant critiques of evolutionary approaches to culture, which are themselves implicated in the naturalizing and legitimizing of social inequalities. It is small wonder that sociocultural anthropologists find it less useful to participate in dialogues with biological anthropologists and archaeologists who employ evolutionary approaches to human diversity than with historians, literary critics, political theorists, philosophers, and cultural geographers.

My point is not that all dialogue—past or present—among the four fields has been rooted in an evolutionist paradigm. A variety of theoretical perspectives (e.g., structural functionalism, structuralism, Marxism, feminist theory), substantive issues, and analytic projects have connected the fields. Nor am I arguing for the exclusion of evolutionary theory or evolutionary studies from the discipline or for the exclusion of "scientific" approaches to the study of culture. The debate over what constitutes "science" in anthropology is a related but different issue from the one I have addressed in this essay. The tendency of some anthropologists to equate evolutionary approaches with "science," however, is a telling indication of its continuing hegemony. It is the disciplinary hegemony of the evolutionist logic that has prescribed the binding together of what Stocking has called the "normative, four subfield discipline" that I have questioned in this essay.

The nationalist and pragmatic arguments for preserving the four-field discipline have had considerable success in sustaining the normative image of a holistic science of anthropology in the United States. Whether sticking together has brought the discipline the promised respect and resources remains in doubt. The question of whether some of the four fields have benefited more than others from the "unity of the discipline" also remains unanswered. The disadvantages—both pragmatic and intellectual—seem clearer. The canonization of the four-field discipline and its underlying evolutionist logic has constrained and stifled the exploration of alternative intellectual alignments. The hegemony of a "holistic science" of humankind has limited debate over the configuration of the discipline to the question of whether the fields should remain united or should separate. Assumed in these discussions are the form and theoretical rationale of their articulation.

Collaboration among the four fields has become increasingly recognized as a foundational myth of the discipline rather than fact. Borofsky concludes on the basis of his survey of articles published in the *American Anthropologist* over the hundred-year period from 1899 to 1999 that "substantive collaboration across anthropological subfields is largely a myth." Only 9.5 percent of the 3,264 articles "bring the discipline's subfields together in significant ways" by drawing substantially "on more than one anthropological subfield in the analysis of their data" (2002, 463). Borofsky's finding that collaborative articles in the decades preceding the 1970s were consistently lower than 9.5 percent, moreover, belies the myth of a disciplinary past in which greater collaboration existed among the four fields. The "golden era" of collaboration—if it can be called that—has ironically been the last three decades (1971–1998), in which the number of collaborative articles climbed higher, most likely because during this period the editors of the *AA* were explicitly committed to integrating the discipline.[14] Even before World War II, Kroeber was the only one of the AAA presidents who "contributed in a substantial way to as many as three of the discipline's four fields" (Stocking 1988, 19). Like most "golden era" narratives, this one more accurately reflects a nostalgic yearning for a nonexistent past than a reliable account of a lost one.

If collaboration among the four fields is largely a myth, what of competition among them? Disagreements over theories, methods, and even the aims of a discipline could, one might argue, be productive and energizing. According to such a "free market" model of scholarly production, intense competition among schools and approaches within a discipline should spur the development of innovative ideas and methods. Whether such a free market of ideas actually operates in the academy depends on whether academic "consumers" act like free market seekers of value. Who these academic consumers are and how their behavior is shaped by academic institutions that constrain their "choices" is unclear. There remains, moreover, the question of what the competing units should be. In other words, we might ask whether the units engaged in this competition should be fields, disciplines, or theoretical alliances that crosscut them. If a free market model of competition works, then we might ask why we should not foster competition among a number of different interdisciplinary articulations. Why should there be a single hegemonic articulation motivated and legitimated by a single hegemonic logic?

Competition among the four fields in anthropology, however, appears to have been more productive of tensions and conflicts over resource distribution than of innovative theories and methods. In sociocultural anthropology, the innovative theoretical and methodological developments of the past quarter century—including reflexive, feminist, poststructuralist, postcolonial, and transnational approaches to culture—were not generated by competition between cultural anthropology and other fields in the discipline; nor were they stimulated by competition with evolutionary approaches to culture. Rather, they were incited by the growing dissatisfaction of sociocultural anthropologists with prevailing forms of cultural theory, including structural-functionalist, economic determinist, psychological, cognitive, and androcentric approaches. This dissatisfaction led us to look beyond the boundaries of the discipline to scholarship in the humanities and other social sciences.

Recent developments in the anthropology of kinship are a case in point. The innovations that have led us from Radcliffe-Brown's structural functionalism to Lévi-Strauss's structuralism, Schneider's symbolic analysis, Bourdieu's practice theory, Foucault's discourse analysis, and feminist gender analysis did not emerge out of competition between biological and cultural theories of kinship but out of competition among varieties of structuralist, interactionist, economic, and interpretive theories of culture and through dialogue between sociocultural anthropologists and scholars in other fields (notably, linguistics, sociology, history, literature, political theory, and feminist theory). Competition between biological and cultural theories of kinship has led to little more than a recycling of a tired and unproductive debate over the determining power of "nature" versus "nurture."

Toward Flexible Disciplinarity

The alternative I propose to the "normative four-subfield discipline" is a nonessentialist, flexible disciplinarity that would enable scholars in each of the four fields to forge innovative intra- and interdisciplinary alliances, assembling a multiplicity of new bundles or, as Clifford (this volume) puts it, "contingent articulations." Anthropology would then operate much as Galison (1997) has described the operation of physics, as a trading zone in which scientists with divergent ways of conceptualizing and organizing the world forge transitory, local languages—pidgins and creoles—to facilitate exchanges, even while disagreeing about the meaning of the items exchanged and their significance in a broader context. One advantage of this metaphor is that it recognizes that fruitful work can proceed in the absence of agreement over methods, theories, epistemologies, or even disciplinary goals. A second advantage is that it figures a discipline as historically sutured and contingent, rather than as defined and delimited by a distinctive subject matter, methodology, or theory. Consequently, it does not privilege intradisciplinary dialogues over interdisciplinary ones but instead fosters the development of creative interdisciplinary alignments. Finally, it does not treat as sacred and timeless a contingent disciplinary articulation that was forged a century ago to meet the intellectual and political challenges of a different historical conjuncture.

NOTES

I would like to thank Don Donham, Akhil Gupta, Rena Lederman, Lisa Rofel, Dan Segal, Mei Zhan, and the anonymous reviewers for their valuable comments and suggestions.

1. In this narrative, the ultimate end to the nightmare of disciplinary balkanization is "what happened at Stanford." In 1998, the Department of Anthropology of Stanford University, which had been formed in the 1950s with a focus on sociocultural anthropology, split into two departments: the Department of Anthropological Sciences and the Department of Cultural and Social Anthropology. Faculty in the original department were given a choice of which new department they would join. I joined and chaired the Department of Cultural and Social Anthropology.

2. Consider, for example, Lewis Henry Morgan's initial interest in fashioning a distinctive American identity by drawing on Native American customs and his reformulation of this into the study of Native American society and social evolutionary theory (Ben-Zvi 2003a, 2003b; Deloria 1998; Feeley-Harnik 2001; Trautmann 1987).

3. See Kuper (1988) for a critique of primitivism and social evolutionism in anthropology.

4. The argument for a four-field discipline of anthropology was not entirely lacking in Britain. See Adams (1998) on the four-field tendencies in turn-of-the-century British anthropology. He notes that "As late as 1909, the Board of Studies in Anthropology at the University of London proposed a guide for the study and teaching of anthropology which embraced physical anthropology and cultural anthropology" (368).

5. The term *settler colonialism* was suggested by the historian David K. Fieldhouse (1982) to distinguish "occupation colonies" from "settlement colonies," including the first European colonies in America.

6. Ben-zvi (2003a, 5) attributes the lack of attention to settler colonialism in U.S. history to five major attitudes of intervention in U.S. culture: distinctions between "national" and "colonial" periods; historiographic emphasis on the nation as a foundational form; tensions that separate "postcolonial studies" or "postcolonial theory" from "colonial studies"; debates about what constitutes postcoloniality and transnationalism in U.S. culture and history; and studies that focus on imperialist expansion as national property.

7. Morgan's scholarship was produced in a period that was dense with works that would prove to be "decisive in the formation of modern anthropology" (Trautmann 1987, 2). In addition to the books by Bachofen, Maine, McLennan, and de Coulange, Darwin's *The Origin of Species* (1859) and *The Descent of Man* (1871) marked the beginning and end of the "long decade" of the 1860s.

8. According to Deloria, this group "met at monthly campfires deep in the New York woods. Garbed in Indian costume, they called one another by Indian names and proffered nostalgic, metaphor-drenched poetry and prose as prototypes of a national literature" (1998, 73).

9. As Stocking (1996, 5) notes, Bunzl's (1996) essay on Boas and the Humboldtian tradition is the first systematic attempt to investigate the connections between Boas's concept of culture and the German intellectual tradition.

10. See also Stocking (1960) on the founding of the AAA.

11. This group had been organized since 1890 in the Anthropology Society of Washington and was the publisher of the *American Anthropologist* (Stocking 1988, 17).

12. Bunzl (1996) views the more "physicalistic aspects" of Boas's early anthropology as an accommodation to his institutional dependency on evolutionary anthropologists for the support of his ethnographic research.

13. Here I part company with Lederman (this volume), who argues that our effectiveness in critiquing racism is enhanced by integrating biological and cultural anthropology. I agree that we should draw on both biological and cultural evidence to demonstrate that race is biologically meaningless but culturally powerful in producing social inequalities. But I do not view this as calling for the integration of biological and cultural anthropology any more than drawing on historical and cultural evidence to document cultural change calls for the integration of history and anthropology in the same discipline.

14. Having made this finding of the myth of four-field disciplinary integration, Borofsky unfortunately contradicts himself by laying the blame on increasing specialization. In an uncritical Durkheimian move, he grants academic specialization a "momentum all its own" and assumes that it leads to intellectual fragmentation, thus replacing the myth of the "golden era" of collaboration with the myth of specialization and fragmentation. He even goes so far as to attribute increasing specialization to the "fragmentation and atomization of modern life" (2002, 472).

Languages/Cultures Are Dead!
Long Live the Linguistic-Cultural!

MICHAEL SILVERSTEIN

There can be no forgetting that disciplines, like dynastic monarchies, go on even in the face of the demise of the old regime and the accession of the new. The formulaic turn of phrase in my title plays upon this characteristic. In what follows, then, I want to trace change and continuity in the way both linguistic and sociocultural anthropologists have looked at their objects of scholarly or scientific investigation. I want to suggest that the social organization of disciplinarity has been very important. There is a long historical sociology of knowledge in which have occurred major realignments of how and where the discipline labeled "anthropology" fits into larger fields of scholarly and scientific enterprise, determining anthropology's connection to them via issues and methodologies, organizations, and personnel. Here, I want especially to point out that changing interdisciplinary connections relate directly to shifts in intradisciplinary configuration—that is, to how various lines of theorization and investigation within anthropology have mutually enriched each other and continue to do so.

By worrying the structures of scientific and scholarly relations, I hope to address the "death" and "life" issues about both anthropology and its objects of description and interpretation. For I hold that these issues of "death" and "life" are, in a sense, matters of perspective that lead anthropologists, in our own time no less than previously, to particular understandings of disciplinary opportunities. At earlier moments in both linguistics and ethnology, our work often seemed to be feverish exercises in the realm of the "death"—and hence increasing dearth—of distinct, classifiable, namable entities, called languages and cultures, in their nominal, projectively "thingy" conceptualization. Reconceptualized from a different perspective, however, our brief is really to understand cultural "life": seeking the essence, as it were, of the linguistic-cultural semiotic—adjectivally conceptualized, we might say. One might argue that it has all along been the distinct brief of anthropology to explore how this produces the sociohistorically emergent properties of human-group social life. Those emergent properties include, interestingly enough, the nominally conceptualized "languages" and "cultures" that anthropologists, as well as ordinary folks, have found so good to think.

The Epistemic Era of Anthropological Typology

Anthropology, like so many of the sciences, was poured out of the Enlightenment cornucopia, though it solidified as a discursive field originally in the image of comparative philology and (universal) culture-history only in the mid- to late nineteenth century.[1] Thus, observe the sweep of history we recuperate to create a captioned image of the "discipline of anthropology," which has moved through intellectual phases both of its own making and as a consequence of larger intellectual currents. After 1859 and the publication of *The Origin of Species*, for example, anthropology contributed centrally to a wider conversation about relations between civilization and "nature." The discourse became increasingly frank in its problematization of human culture-history along lines of "race," which could now be seen as the intra-species correspondent to the now Darwinian evolutionary biologism in discourse about the wider domain of all life forms.[2]

But what is interesting here is that such a discourse is recognizable within a much longer phase of anthropology of reasonable stability and duration, an epistemic era characterizable in its general outlines, in which the field could be conceptualized very much like taxonomy-centered (and eventually evolutionary) zoological and botanical science. In such a field, classification and its explanation drove empirical engagement with the stuff of anthropological work and connected the observed diversity of "cultures" and "languages" of "populations" and "communities" to theorizing what lay behind the nodes of the classification. Thus, what is (or was) the significance of the "Turanian" mode of kinship classification of a society that might be revealed through a study of how its language's kinship lexemes group or cluster genealogical denotata?

Posing the question itself presupposes that there are principles of classification underlying kinterminological systems and that genealogically described exemplars can be assigned to one or another of the terminological categories as they are encountered. More important, the question presupposes that there is some framework in which these facts, comprised of particular terminologies-in-societies, are themselves instances within a typology of categorizations. The typology should be consistent with, or at least not contradictory to, some interpretative scheme that theorizes the variation observed in classificatory systems and, based on this, interprets or explains the variation predicted to be possible. For kinship studies at one time, for example, it was assumed that there exists a universal evolutionary tendency manifest in the ways humans conceptualize their normative domestic social arrangements and how speakers of languages denote them in expressions grammatically formed from terminologized primes. So a kind of typological sequence was indicated, in turn indicative of the story of humankind's social-conceptual, not to say moral, evolution.[3] Now straightforward evolutionism has been, perforce, mostly abandoned within anthropology, certainly within sociocultural anthropology. And structural linguistic theory (not to say philosophy of mind, language, and science) has definitively nullified attempts to study denotation by merely studying simple words as names for clumped or grouped denotata (the "nomenclaturist" view of language ridiculed by Saussure). Yet, we should note, the study of kinship terminological systems fashioned under these very two exploded commitments remained central to anthropology for a good part of the twentieth century as the discipline moved beyond them, because it constituted a lens of classificatory typological gaze.

Explanatory theorizing both underpins scientific typology in such an episteme and presupposes that the phenomena typologized constitute its field of empirical validation. In anthropology, we have had positive typological science, first as social evolutionism in a diachronic framework and later as it turned into evolutionism's synchronicist counterpart, (structural-) functionalism. We have also had negative theorizing, as in Boasian cosmographic historicism and its synchronicist counterpart, culturological (symbols-and-) meaningism. These four general approaches to dealing with typological and classificatory data have in fact arisen in an interesting dialectic more or less across the Atlantic, as first positive then dialectically negative treatments of typological variation and its interpretability.

Social evolutionism, in particular universal schemes of humanity-wide transformation, emerged primarily in European anthropological theorizing during the late nineteenth century. Typological placement of social custom and belief within such schemes of transformation thus implies that there are contemporary "species" of humanity that, all the while our coevals, are more and less similar to ancestral type, having to lesser or greater degree changed over evolutionary time. Notice how, when treated as social "traits" that can cluster—cf. Tylor's (1888) method of adhesions—typological facts of particular societies can be arrayed into the dimensions of a unified and universal multivariate space of possibilities. In response to this, Boasian cosmographic historicism, telling endlessly varied narratives of how "traits" came to be associated—to cluster—through local historical process, rendered problematic such universal typologies. In this view Tylorian adhesions seem to have emerged over prehistorical as well as historical time in different societies in very particular ways. Such multiple histories render suspect the presumed universal transitions-across-type postulated by such positive approaches—those relying on one key typological factor (Morgan or Marx) or those based on a multivariate space (Tylor, Spencer).[4]

Also problematic is evolution's synchronicized counterpart in social anthropology, the way that typological variation is related to "function" in the theoretical lineage from Durkheim through Radcliffe-Brown and beyond.[5] Seen as the parts of a morphology of social norms—of a social structure abstracted from time—each typological fact about social practices can be evaluated for its contribution to the "timeless" sustainable functioning of an encompassing social order. Such principles of contributory functionality can, of course, be generalized across "species" of the genus "society," so that implied here is a mode of comparing social practices typologically just as much as in evolutionism.[6] In structural-functionalism, putatively universal functional requirements on social arrangements, such as an incest taboo, the unity of sibling groups, and other general "functional" principles, intersect in the morphology of social groups. In explanatory interpretation of the typological facts, we attempt to show how particular intersections of typological features "solve" the problems of self-sustenance for social formations, vicissitudes of social organizational perturbations in real time notwithstanding.[7]

This synchronicist functionalism was highly influential in America, especially when it morphed into a "social anthropology" cognizant as well of Parsonian sociological functionalism. And this American social anthropology itself found its negative counterpart in what I call "symbols-and-meaningism," in which anthropology becomes a hermeneutic rather than an observational science. As noted, in functionalist thought typologies and the interpretative principles for organizing our understanding of the species of the genus "society" depend on comparing customs—institutions of people's mutually calibrated social behavior—that are recognizable as comparable in particular respects by their place within a sustainable social order. We might argue, by contrast—as theorists such as Geertz (1973) and Schneider (1968, 1984) and their students have forcefully done—that one cannot find any truly cross-culturally comparable social practices to observe and notate in the *Notes and Queries* social anthropological manner. For people at least implicitly understand all of the varied practices and events of their lives together against norms of significance deriving from very local systems of "meaningfulness." Then our accounts of such highly local "cultural" conceptualizations—though perhaps focused on seemingly "same" practices—have, mutatis mutandis, all the extraordinary variability of Boasian historicist narratives, only here in the synchronic or functional realm. So for symbols-and-meaningism, social practices as such become, once more, only apparently "the same" as we move from social group to social group; if local significance or "meanings" differ, then social practices cannot be considered comparable.

Whether one sees this as a semiotic or semiological turn of anthropology or a turn to interpretivism or hermeneutics—these and other counterstructural-functional self-captionings have all been at one or another time used—the point of all of them is that meaning, not social morphology, rules. And meaning is infinitely subtle and variable, endlessly defeasible, and doggone hard to find if one has not a clue as to what one might mean by "meaning," as alas many of the writers in these modes do not. So, taken at its most extreme literalness, we have here potentially a kind of nihilism about the very possibility of comparison of social forms like "kinship" practices, about our very ability to understand something of a culture not one's own (and, derivatively, the social practices made meaningful in respect of it). Can we even say that a particular "meaning"-infused social practice is not the same as some other if all knowledge on which anthropology might rest is ineluctably "local" in character? It is no wonder that precisely in the contemplation of this disciplinary epistemological abyss, the divide between sciences and humanities, on the one hand, and/or modernism and postmodernism, on the other, is invoked in some combination by various writers seeking to clarify what is at stake.[8]

Anthropology among the Disciplinary "Sciences"

In this roughly sketched intellectual history of four dialectical moments, let us turn to anthropology's position in the configuration of sciences. This might be addressed in terms of two dimensions, substantive issues and methodological/theoretical style.

With respect to substantive issues, its connection to other sciences was through issues held in common, about which anthropology's particular data constitute either support for or challenges to other fields' results, its data constituting usable evidence that can be integrated into these other theoretical discourses. Here, think for example of anthropology's relationship to comparative vertebrate anatomy and its evolutionary interpretation including human paleontology. The physical data of cranial and other skeletal measures, the evidence of growth curves of the body's morphology, and so forth can be read across species, one of them *Homo sapiens* (*sapiens*). The contemporary period of "the double helix" operates similarly at the level of molecular biological comparison.

Again, think of anthropology's relationship to both species-specific cognitive psychology—cf. the "psychic unity" doctrine in the face of cultural and linguistic diversity—and comparative and even "evolutionary" psychology (a.k.a. sociobiology; cf. n. 3). We can make inferences about cognitive groupings or categorizations of things and people that are, minimally, implicit in social practices or, maximally, both experienced and representationally explicit (for example, in language forms or even in elaborate theoretical discourses about the universe of imaginable "reality" that theorize and explain the existence of such categorizations, as in all ["ethno"-]science). We can register variation across societies in the normative social practices that depend on how individuals from different social categories are recruited to role. We can as well register variation in societies' texts of verbal and other representational sorts.[9]

In general, what is of concern is the impact of the fact of humans' possession of culture and language—that is, our possession of specific, diverse but equivalently rich cultures and languages—on the presumed psychological and biological substrate of this species, among others. Thus note that everything from the comparative study of the ability of humans and other primates to learn to communicate in "language" to the study of the relation of color perception to color as a possibly culturalized experience can be seen in this framework.[10] Even various norms of human interpersonal behavior in social context, mediated as they are by verbal and other communication, can be seen in relation to, and perhaps as a kind of continuation-and-analogue (i.e., homologue) of, animal ethology. Thus, social practice as conventionally normed social cognition among humans is frequently compared to ethological behavior of other species, reading these practices across species at least as analogues, sometimes to make the "evolutionary psychological" argument that they are homologues.

These substantive connections readily resonate with popular expression in the American and other media publics, which, using results of anthropology, are ever ready excitedly to imagine the "animal" lurking within every human as much as, projecting, to appreciate the humanlike "soul" within every animal. Whether this happens under the banner of "sociobiology" or "evolutionary psychology," anthropology is summoned to these discourses to provide data interpretable in the terms demanded. Hence, anthropology gets summoned to reduce human facts of what looks like conventions of meaningfulness to facts of functionality within some synchronic or diachronic scheme of such, so as to make them appear comparable to facts of animal ethology: (human) bodily stance and (animal) mating displays are perennial favorites, for example. Or anthropology is summoned to witness facts of animal ethology—for example, what is called "altruism" or "tool-making" behavior—being reread as similar in kind to those of sociohistorically specific human social action.[11]

With respect to methodological and theoretical style, anthropology's connections to other sciences have been through the mechanism of what I term metaphorical calques, borrowed influences and conceptual shapes gained from familiarity with, if not real knowledge of, these other fields. What results are point-for-point correspondences with other fields in the ways in which anthropologists go about conceptualizing their particular empirical materials so as to draw interpretative conclusions from them. A methodological calque treats data just like those of another field; a theoretical calque sees point-for-point similarity in conceptual frameworks giving significance to such data.

Here, think again of the obvious parallel in an older anthropology between approaches to cultures and languages in the ethnological and linguistic realms as holistic units of some kind and approaches to species in the biological realm. Think then of the implicated theoretical question of how observed diversity arises of cultures and languages. This is frequently seen in relation to the speciation process that explains why diverse but closely related species are observed in natural biomes somewhat isolated one from another in geography or niche.

Both a cultural and linguistic "ecology," more or less calqued from the biological, are implied, mutatis mutandis, by this theoretical and methodological comparison. And indeed, within sociocultural anthropology, cultural ecology captioned as such has long been a staple of everything from Julian Steward's (1955) attempts to nudge Boasian historicism in the direction of "multilinear evolution" to various cybernetic materialisms that read social practices directly as responses to adaptive pressures from positive or negative natural-environmental feedback.

For language, the field of "dialect geography" once constituted an ecological calque in the discourse of historical linguistics. Here, a relationship was drawn between geographical dialects, separated by significant "lines of communicative weakness" (cf. rates of interbreeding) and incipient speciation as viewed in an older, taxon-focused biological science. Separate dialects are thus viewed as "languages in the making" on the order of the relation between biological varieties and separate species.[12] The Weinreich-Labov tradition of sociolinguistics (Weinreich 1954; Weinreich, Labov, and Herzog 1968; Labov 1972, 2001) has renewed and reconceptualized this older dialect geography (cf. Gumperz 1968) along the lines of studying social differentiation within language populations, in effect turning it into a "sociolectology." Ironically, however, such study demonstrates that rather than along lines of weakness of communication, meaningful "-lectal" differentiation seems to reach maximal expression in social formations where people are in dense and obtrusive closeness one to another as members of sociocultural categories. People are observed verbally to differentiate the social positions they inhabit through indexically loaded differences of their language, as demonstrated in Labov's classic New York City neighborhood studies (1972) and many, many others following in their image (see also Bourdieu 1991, 35–102). So there remains a great gap between such meaningful differentiation of language varieties as observed and what is postulated theoretically by the traditional ecological calque of linguistic "speciation."

To think further about methodological calques, consider how, after the demise of unilinear social evolutionism, social anthropologists once looked at the question of the finite diversity of kinship. Of course, such study was based on the existence of paradigmatic structures of simplex kinship lexemes in language (vulgarly, "kinship terminological systems") and how individuals' genealogies can be reckoned in terms of them. In our comparative studies of such systems, by abduction we can construct fundamental explanatory dimensions—for example, genealogical categorization—that would allow us to comprehend why there are limits to typological variability. In this way, we might explain such principles as bifurcation of "parallel" and "cross" kintypes with respect to an ego (Lounsbury 1969b [1964], 202) and other observable typological cleavages. The intersection of all such dimensionalized possibilities would constitute a space for all the attested—and systematically possible—systems of kin classification. Systems would thus fall into types in an orderly way, and competing explanatory motivations for the existence of such types—for example, a "Crow" type, a "Dravidian" type, etc.—at one point did, indeed, fill the journal pages.

Such an approach should be seen in relation to the way, in chemistry, one can now start with the periodic table of elements, a typology of classes of chemical elements worked out by Mendeleev. It is organized around atomic number and, as it has turned out, greater and greater degrees of saturation by electrons of the available positions in greater and greater numbers of orbital positions around the nucleus of an atom (the "explanation" of the Mendeleev typology thus being the gradiently and iteratively instantiated principles that have, in effect, perfected the Bohr atomic model). It predicts observable and theoretically possible kinds of molecules—let alone new elements—on the basis of commonalties of types of atoms in their combinatory potentials under a principled model of the atom. Lévi-Strauss (1958, 1973), of course, has made the intriguing comparison (calque?) of "the atom of kinship," as he has also theorized certain "elementary forms" of how these "atoms" underlie a whole—molecular or crystalline—social structure. In effect, then, elementary society rests on a combinatorics held together by affinal relations that are established in structural time across otherwise incestuous consanguineal clumps or lattices of like "atoms"—for example, unilineal corporate groups. In this truly structural-functional line of explanation, social anthropologists have sought to explain typologies of kin reckoning. Different types become variant, ultimately functionally equivalent expressions of the avoidance of incest and the norms for transfer of (rights in or to) women/goods among corporate kinship groups.[13] One can, of course, go on to study if all of the comparably "molecular" social types based on particular combinatoric principles have further correlative similarities, by degrees, as classes of compounds would in chemistry (potassium chloride and strontium fluoride, for example, constituted analogously in Mendeleevan terms). This work has not been systematically attempted in social anthropology, however. New calques have emerged, as well as new doubts about the very project.

Observe further how certain approaches in anthropology—for example, so-called "ethnoscience" or "cognitive anthropology" or so-called "structural anthropology" (only partially distinguishable from sociological structural functionalism) or "symbolic anthropology"—have also heavily calqued certain structuralist approaches to phonology or phonemics within mid-twentieth-century linguistics, the structural-functional study of sound as it contributes to how language is a denotational system.[14]

Now in one sense phonological facts are indeed facts of the "imposition of culture in nature," a substantive connection of the conventional and cultural to a clearly universal psychological substrate, our general human ability to process articulate sound under a strictly syllabic criterion of phonation and audition. Investigating such phenomena, we can ask substantive questions about how the fundamentally anthropological facts of variation across sound systems in the languages of the world do or do not have some import for psychic unity doctrines. Here is signal success with a method in the analysis of cultural material—language structure—that has implications for questions of a substantive sort posed within psychology and biology. We can use phonetics-phonology to inquire about categorization, about the relations of structural categoricals to the essentially statistical quality of behavioral and perceptual realization of categories, about the robustness of categories across populations of users, etc.[15]

With comparable intent, then, these types of methodological and theoretical calques have sought to duplicate the strategy of phonological analysis both within language (in studying lexical meaning) and outside of it (in the realm of symbols in general). Within language, the question is to what extent the higher, meaning-bearing organization of lexicon in the Saussurean sense can be approached like a system of meaning-differentiating but nonspecifically meaningful combinatoric "-emic" units like phonemes or their implied dimensions of differentiation, the distinctive features.

In the realm of kinship terms, application of a methodological calque of phonemic analysis does not actually work in general, save for a preselected domain of egocentrically reckoned genealogical categories that are recursively saturated by lexemic coding (as opposed to grammatical constructions with iterated possessive constructions). For just in such a realm of denotation do the typologies continue to hold that were worked out—as various "classificatory" types of kinship systems—during the nineteenth century. Thus, at best, once we are given—by hypothesis—a denotational domain of kintypes structured by rules of egocentric genealogical relationship in the usual fashion, we can model the conformity of the limited number of lexemic coding systems found. We cannot in this way inductively "discover" that this or any semantic structure is universally based on genealogy, however, for reasons it would take us far afield to lay out.[16]

At the same time, outside of language, the question is to what extent, if at all, the very nonlinguistic aspects of culture might have these same properties of phonology-like systematicity. In the realm of phonology itself, it should be remembered, the specifically Saussurean properties of phonemes—"sound segments" in our current parlance—their *syntagmatic-combining* properties, derive from how they occur in linear relation one to another within a relatively simple structure, the syllable. So the English form written *cat* is "three segments (phonemes) long"—thus: k—æ—t, in that order. Possible syllable types differ greatly from language to language (a monosyllabic word like Kiksht [Chinookan] *ɬʼtpčkʷt* "it is coming hither out of the water"—with initial stress—would not be countenanced in English!). Yet it is the universal conformity of systems to implicational rules couched in terms of classificatory or *paradigmatic-categorizing* properties that was so successfully developed for phonology, especially by Praguean theorists (of whom Jakobson survived to bring these ideas to America and later—both personally and by proxy—to Paris). The very comparability of two languages with different syllable canons derives, in this view, precisely from the fact that these units defined—structural-functionally—by combinatoric rules correspond, along multiple dimensions (called their "features"), to modes of categorial grouping based ultimately in recurrent—"functional"—properties of actual, perceivable sound-in-the-world (articulo-acoustico-auditory realities) insofar as independently describable.

Now consider a nonlinguistic calque of this kind of phenomenon. How do we manage the analytic extraction of such units, correspondingly syntagmatic and paradigmatic, from sociocultural practices more generally? How do we discern the combinatoric dimensions of sociocultural phenomena, for example, other than perhaps to recognize them, as does Geertz (1973), to be texts? And how do we comprehend the typological variation of systems of "emic" units of culture at the same time as we ground such systems within truly universal real-world phenomena (like sound, for phonological emics; like orderly domains of conceptualizables for lexicological and constructional emics)?

If the goal is to achieve something akin to actual phonological theory, this whole approach has remained a highly problematic enterprise, and for good reason: it is at best a misleading calque in the first place. Many writers have made claims to have found phonemelike "emic" units of which "culture" is said to consist. They have described cultures with values along dimensions of contrast like distinctive features of phonology (that can be represented, under assumptions of their binary quantization, with the familiar pluses and minuses or ones and zeroes). But I would claim that the analytic triumph is dubious at best, since there is no general framework in which these claims make sense so as to ground a culturological "-emics" in the extensionalizable comparatism the phonological or phonemic calque—or its lexicological derivative—presupposes.[17]

My purpose, however, is not to elaborate a critique of cognitivist or structuralist or symbolic approaches to anthropological analysis. My purpose is to point up the methodological calques at work in these projects, which presume upon the model of an isolatable language system—a *langue*—in the Saussurean construal of the matter, even though it is language-in-use—a socioculturally inflected *parole*—that makes of language a substantive part and parcel of culture, as well as a more fruitful exemplar of the cultural and a guide into it. Within such a Saussurean view of language, analysis of a phonemic/phonological system presumes that we can unproblematically draw the boundaries of a language as a "natural," yet at once sociocentric and "mental," object. So calques in other cultural realms make more or less similar presumptions. Yet the yield for such presumptuousness has been at best small, at worst seriously misleading for what one might address as phenomena of "culture," let alone of "language" itself.

In fact, I would claim, down to the recent past the various kinds of anthropological theorizing in respect of cultures and languages have been sorely unnerved, theoretically exercised, even frustrated, when the facts that appeared to empirical view lacked the qualities sought through such isolatable units. Such approaches constitute a museologically or taxonomically inspired enterprise, as we have seen; they imply as a constant of anthropological work a framework of interpretation or explanation for observed variability that orders it in the display cases of our science. Over the years we can follow the move through "traits," "typologies," "functions," "meanings," "oppositional structures," and so forth that have been the foci of analytic rigor in the cultural and linguistic spheres of factuality, as though anthropologists were discovering these to be factual attributes of species of flora and fauna.

Yet what to do? The people clamor for "pure" languages and cultures that they can order into some—cultural!—scheme. Official and governmental institutions do so even more insistently for their own political reasons. Yet cumulating almost from the beginning of disciplinary anthropology, the methods of discernment brought to bear on "cultures" and "languages" have revealed acculturation and assimilation and hybridity; then perhaps anthropological descriptions have attempted to conceal (or at least theoretically to "normalize" for) the *realia* encountered. Observation in tension with classificatory theorizing has revealed/concealed multilingual speakers in plurilingual communities, pidgin and creole languages, and other abominations of classification of isolatable systems. What then is the reality of what have seemed—to "natives" no less and perhaps more than to anthropologists and linguists—to be bounded, countable, mappable cultures and languages in mutually reinforcing social aggregation? Are these the discrete and "shared" attributes of groups of people in ways that can be revealed to empirical investigation?

Here is our jittery state in respect of the obscure objects of scientific desire: has it been our frameworks, our empirical and analytic methods, our connections to discourses both disciplinary and beyond that make this seem unlikely of realization? Or is it the phenomena themselves that really have materially changed, even disappeared, over the last century of typologically informed anthropology? Where is the point of view located from which such questions can be at least asked, if not answered?

Sociocultural anthropology has moved itself, very self-consciously, beyond the unquestioning taxonomic era, with input from several intellectual trends both inside the discipline and outside of it. Part of the transition has even involved anthropologists in "culture wars"—in two senses—and "science wars" of our own kind and making, as the consequences became clear to both proponents and opponents of abandoning the earlier framing presuppositions.[18] This larger trend in sociocultural anthropology encompasses many moments, in which concepts of culture and social structure and practice have been repeatedly interrogated, especially to see of what use they are to projects of various sorts—"-isms" and "-ities"—from the frankly political to the philosophical. What has emerged from anthropology's new encounters with feminism, Marxism, historicism, materialism, deconstructionism, antifoundational perspectivalism, subalter(n)ity, reflexivity, and so forth is a suspiciousness of the very locatability—in empirical "reality," as well as in a stable analytic—of thingy, boundable wholes called languages and cultures that were once at the epistemic center of the field.

Who these days can straightforwardly—and with straight face—compare Culture A with Culture B, or Language C with Language D? What if these are *not* all phenomena that remain stably and coherently observable to the dispassionate, inquiring scientific cognition in the objective way previously assumed—even were the linguistic and the cultural approached by well-intentioned, left-liberal, relativist comparatists who are philosophically savvy practitioners of disinterested abstraction and extraction? What if, indeed?

But I would not want us to see in these developments the demise of something wonderful, a long-standing epistemic way of disinterestedly knowing humanity assaulted and brought to naught by the wounds of a thousand interested (i.e., not disinterested) critical plaints. I would see these questions actually to be attempts from many sides to go beyond mere lip-service as anthropologists to the serious (re)discovery that "meaning" is at the center of language and culture. The (re)discovery is serious enough to begin to unravel the previously sacred bundle of subfields and hence to refashion an alternate, even wider, connectedness of anthropology to yet other fields—history, politics, currents in philosophy and literature, etc.[19]

Let us recall that by the mid-1960s Chomskian ideas widely diffused in the behavioral and social sciences. These had been developed, ironically enough, for isolatable grammatical structures of languages and for the "universal grammar" hypothesized to underlie all such human grammars. Beyond the specific formal approach to grammar itself, however, here was once more an anti-evolutionary celebration of the organized, distinctively human faculties in linguistic and other higher cognition—certainly emboldening sociocultural anthropology (in America and beyond) to reenter a larger, somewhat newly conceptualized field of discourse about our distinctively (and seemingly biologically discontinuous) "human nature" as something involving human understanding.

Culture, too, then being thought of by at least one major cluster of theorists as a group's sociohistorically specific and normative "symbols and meanings," a sui generis principle in people's lives, the manner of operation of this principle came once more to the fore in a new way. To be sure, this self-styled "symbolic anthropology" constituted at once the projective hypostatizing of an abstract essence underlying the individuation of local groups by virtue of "having a culture" (cf. Herder).[20] But as external and reflexive critique of such notions ruminatively worked itself out, symbolic anthropology as a disciplinary movement in fact constituted the first stage of giving up the older museology of cultural and linguistic forms in anthropological theorizing.

For sociocultural work has ever since this turn been decreasingly concerned with a partitioning of whole cultures that have been or can be assigned to groups of people as a kind of primary possession or attribute. Increasingly anthropologists have been concerned with explaining how semiotic (a.k.a. "symbolic") forms could be locally meaningful in a specifically human and group-relevant way, even subject to contention and dispute within groups. The best of such work sees that "the native's point of view"—in Malinowski's (1922, 25) phrasing—is always emergent within the framework of local structures of meaningfulness. This dialectically becomes immanent in—presupposed by and emergent from—people's praxis and consciousness in certain conditions of group life. But how did we get from "symbolic anthropology" to such a *semiotic praxiology*, even though, as we have seen, along the way there has been much in anthropologists' uses of concepts of meaning that is simplistic and miscalqued from linguistics, among the semiotic sciences? Here I think all the -isms and -ities are very much to the point.

Consider such indicators as Sherry Ortner's mid-1980s bellwether piece (1984) on what she terms "practice" anthropology, or what we might rather term "process anthropology": it in essence declares the end of the museological era in the study of culture. Interestingly, Ortner's essay does not explicitly articulate the shape of an anthropology of semiotic praxis, in which concepts like "culture" and "language" would have a definite, if new, place. It articulates the necessity for such an anthropology, as what "symbolic anthropology" then was becoming in various guises, in response to the various kinds of -ist, and -itical critiques. Indeed, all of these critical stances looked to connect both micro- and macro-level causes and effects—sociopolitical, socioeconomic, sociohistorical—to "symbols," in effect negating the very apolitical, noneconomic, unhistorical abstraction that in their most extreme form the earlier calques of "meaning" implied about anthropology's stance toward culture. But in such a theoretical transmutation does "culture" have to become normative ideology-as-false-consciousness? Does it have to be swept up in a necessarily "pejorative" reading (Geuss 1981, 12–22) in respect of clashes of group power, wealth/status, and memory? Ortner (1984, 147), for one, coding it with ancestral emblems as topoi, seems to look to a happy theoretical blending of Weber and Marx as the path forward.

In fact, I would maintain, already by this time "symbolic anthropology" had moved most definitely toward discourse (in the expanding denotation of the term), especially in those theorizing milieus that had already been conducive to learning from advances made in shaping a new linguistic anthropology. For there emerged a new connection between sociocultural anthropology and a linguistics outside of the doctrinal Chomskian orbit, one in which, certainly during the period from the mid-1960s (Gumperz and Hymes 1964, 1972; Bright 1966) to the mid-1970s, a semiotic praxis orientation had been invented—the "pragmatics," as it were, of language-in-use, both as a cultural prototype and as the cultural medium par excellence.

And it has been through such an anthropology of praxis that one can now see that the very concepts of stable "cultures" and "languages" are ideological constructs that have their own sociocultural conditions of viability. That is not to say that languages and cultures are not "real"; indeed, they are very real, though just not the kind of natural objects upon the existence or boundaries or essence of which anthropological theories in all of the subfields of the museological era have depended.

Languages and cultures are emergent phenomena of sociocultural process, unstable and sociohistorically contingent as they are themselves invoked by "the natives" as a contributory part—a moment— of a dialectical process of politicoeconomically and historically specific meaning making.[21] And it is not only "the natives" who are interested. One can, moreover, see that these concepts, now reflexively taken up for conceptual critique by sociocultural and linguistic anthropology, have already been assimilated into various transnational or "global," nation-statist, ethnonationalist, and other yet more circumscribedly "local" projects of one or another identifiable social interest.[22]

We might term our current state of theorizing in sociocultural and linguistic anthropology as "postprocessual," then, to borrow from our archaeological colleagues. That is, having brought together semiotic praxis orientation with its inevitable deconstruction of the very museological concepts of "language" and "culture"—which are seen retrospectively to have been reflexive ideological moves—we understand the situation to be something like the following. The very subject matter of nineteenth-century linguistics and sociocultural anthropology ("ethnology"), languages and cultures, constitutes to a large extent emergent constructions of various kinds of sociohistorical institutionalizations of interests—colonial, (ethno)nationalist and nation-statist, class, etc., to name a few basic intersecting dimensions. What have emerged institutionally in European and derivative social formations as the disciplines of linguistics and anthropology have, perforce, become enmeshed in these constructions in complex ways. So as we reflexively read against these forces and influences, our problem with languages as with cultures is to theorize this state of always emergent production *from the inside*, as it were, starting from a consciousness of the sociohistorical institutionalizations in which the discipline or its subdisciplines have emerged.

Our Disappearing—or Proper?—Subject Matter

All this intellectual history we still live with, enmeshed as we are in a process of which a properly reflexive historical sociology of knowledge is yet to be definitively written. Our consciousness as anthropologists, as well as citizens, about our subject matter is shaped by this historical sociology. So my point is this: the image of "disappearing" or—to use the colorless Green idea—"endangered" languages and cultures is really a

duplex one, produced perhaps as much by the change in our consciousness of the way we go about doing linguistic and sociocultural anthropology as by any forces of globalizing homogenization now dramatically
accelerating mass uniformity.[23]

Once upon a time, we have said, scholars worried about the possibility
of documentation of a language or a culture complete enough for placement in a taxonomic scheme, whether typological or historical. We worried about refinements of method and theory up to the most exacting
standards for these tasks, feeling that we "knew" our linguistic and cultural material to the extent we met and exceeded these needs. Countable,
classifiable languages were once understood for such purposes as collections of words and expressions, lexical handles on a unique treasurehouse
of Lockean "ethno"-concepts and therefore the possession of a bounded
and uniquely classifiable people-with-a-culture, whose dictionary was a
travel guide "from the natives' point of view." We now worry about how
the images of *a* language or *a* culture are themselves constituted as meaningful realities within the scheme of normative subjectivity of a population of one or another sort. We expect that languages and cultures are
always in some only relatively stable phase of a dialectics of formation
and dissolution along multiple dimensions, and we appreciate that they
are permeable one to another in interesting ways, producing new conditions of "the linguistic" and "the cultural."

Within linguistic anthropology, for example, many of us have studied
historical linguistic processes of jargonization—pidginization—creolization—decreolization as the "life cycle" of contact-induced change and its
localizing aftermath.[24] Communicating across language communities,
people develop first lexical-phraseological means of routinizing discursive
interaction—for example, commercial jargons—and then a grammatically
reduced auxiliary language emerges under certain social conditions, frequently recognizable as, or at least thought to be, a pidginized form of one
of the languages concerned: a grammatically stable pidgin. If this language becomes a true first language or mother tongue, it reaches a systematicity of a new sort as a so-called creole, frequently within a larger,
plurilingual speech community. In many cases, a creole is historically
related to another language in a relationship of sociocultural stratifica-
tion—perhaps (though not always) the very language the pidginized form
of which was used in the contact community—that sets up a trajectory of
decreolization. Such processes certainly appear in the historical record of

European exploration, trade, colonialism, and their aftermath. And we are able as well to discern these processes in ancient and non-European situations as well, as for example in the spread of languages of culture in Africa, Asia, and the pre-Columbian Western Hemisphere.

Observe that wherever we look to actual processes of linguistic history in conditions of contact, this begins to look more and more like the norm in the whole wider world of languages, as of cultures. The taxonomically and museologically teratological have thus become the very expected case of the postprocessualist view—the view of "language"s and "culture"s in the contemporary state. Observe that once upon a time pidgin and creole languages presented grave problems for taxonomy because they are historically emergent as communicational solutions in situations that at least started as prolonged and stable contact across language communities. Which single language could be their "parent" system, as it were? With which language system's actual forms are the forms of a pidgin or a creole language continuous in the way that we understand historical continuity in the classifying mode? We frequently find that there are grammatical features of one language and lexical features of a second clearly to be discerned in such languages that result from contact.[25]

This is not to deny the empirical fact that there are increasingly powerful politicoeconomic forces that ever more efficiently and directly interfere with the modes of autonomous "localization" of language and culture in relatively small-scale groups (see Silverstein 1998, referencing Appadurai 1996, 178–199). These processes of decreased autonomy of localization—of the internally normativized social distribution of linguistic and cultural form—emerge to the post-Herderian consciousness of linguists and anthropologists no less than of nonscholars as "language loss" and "culture loss," to be sure. And in the interpreting descriptive calque of post-Herderian anthropology, these nodes of our taxonomic trees of difference do indeed become extinct as autonomously localized languages/ cultures.

But at the same time there is increased complexity in the variation of the linguistic and cultural over a larger population linked to some larger-scale processes that may seem to have obliterated the local "language" and/or "culture." This emerges to analytic light as the making of microvariation within politicoeconomically larger-scale units. It is a new and emergent fact of descriptive life somewhat jolting to the taxonomic and museological views—as were the discovery of pidginization and creolization phenomena to earlier students of language history. But theoretically we must reckon with these facts of integrated variation in much the same terms as the more subtle and processual treatment of difference of languages/cultures has begun to reckon with the constructivity of languages and cultures in the older sense.

Indeed, think on the historical plane of how Roman Latin of the Julian and Augustan imperium became locally differentiated in geopolitical ways that yield only a millennium later to processes of nation-state standardization—sometimes, as for contemporary Sardinian or Provençal, only lingering regional-ethnonationalist attempts—as what we now know to call each of the separate Romance languages (Meillet 1922, 305–322; 1936, 90–122; Elcock 1960). Each more originally "local" and autonomous Celtic, Iberian, or other language of various local groups had been in a state of contact, bilingualism, creolization even, with Latin over a long period of time. Hence, we must seek the historical trace of how the Romance languages came into being as "languages" in processes that start with the spread into contact situations of Latin itself over long spans of dialectic time. As Latin itself, in more or less its classical form, survived alongside the emerging Romance languages (plus others) all over Europe, so also Greek, Sanskrit, Arabic, Persian, several Chinese languages, and others have served as integrative frameworks for comparable developments elsewhere at one or another time. It is not far to think of the comparable case today of English, spreading globally in various situations of contact, plurilingualism, and pidginization/creolization in one or another local social formation where Anglophony mediates at least some aspects of local cultural phenomena.

So these phenomena demonstrate once and for all that the facts of what looked like "speciation" of distinct languages and cultures are not, as it were, "natural" facts. They are, first, sociocultural facts. Second, they are therefore facts of normativities that underlie meaning-in-praxis, relative to which groupness is constituted, maintained, and transformed. How extraordinarily more problematic are any arguments comparing human groupness and other kinds, such as found in the biotic world, notwithstanding the fact that humans are a biological species!

Even if we now see more clearly within the discipline of anthropology the incorrectness of the earlier assumptions of what I have termed the taxonomic and museological era, there are ironies involved. The contemporary condition in which the linguistic and cultural exist is, in fact, partly a result of what I have termed the taxonomizing and museologizing traditions of linguistics and anthropology. Knowledge produced in that tradition has both emerged from and become inextricably intertwined with reflexive consciousness of language users as sociocultural beings. In this way, people come to a realization of their groupness as a function of the emblematic status of markers of difference of "language" and "culture," diacritics of an individual's belonging as well as of a group's distinctness.[26]

In the contemporary world, sociocultural process produces differentiation of *a* language and *a* culture as a vital aspect of an individual's group membership and of a group's differential identity relative to others. But we need not therefore accept these terms as unanalyzable. Indeed, to penetrate the "cultures of language" and the "politics of 'culture'" by which is produced what Appadurai (1996) has called the essential "locality" of communities in the face of boundary-breaching (or at least boundary-problematizing) forces is perhaps the central contemporary task of linguistic and sociocultural anthropology. Interestingly enough, when we view cultural phenomena more generally, precisely this postprocessual approach we take has a common conceptual vocabulary and mode of approach. It is no coincidence, therefore, to say that linguistic anthropology *is* sociocultural anthropology with a twist, the theoretical as well as instrumental (via "discourse" or "the discursive") worrying of our same basic data, semiosis in various orders of contextualization. The results of such theoretical and methodological commonality our less linguistic and more sociocultural brethren have been readily absorbing into the field more generally for some time—and, let us hope, for some time to come.

NOTES

1. In this essay, I can only gesture to the necessity of bringing together all of the following in order to tell this story: (1) the historical sociology of semiotic ideas in ever more encompassing circulation gradually moving forward from the seventeenth century Baconians (and Descartes); (2) the history of institutions that dialectically correspond to and shape such circulation, e.g., the sites of emerging disciplinarity as such—learned, scientific, and pedagogical institutions, among numerous others; and (3) the specific intra- and interdisciplinary, issue-focused conversations constituting the historical flow of scholarly and scientific work we recuperate as we look backward from where we are now situated, creating our "disciplinary history" as a mode of our own historical consciousness. Some exemplary initial orientations to various critical aspects of this complex phenomenon are in Aarsleff (1982); Sahlins (2000a); Stocking (1968, 1987, 1995);

Morpurgo-Davies (1994); Trautmann (1997); Shapin (1994); and Stillman (1995), among others.

2. A century later, to many sociocultural anthropologists the advent of sociobiology (Wilson 1975, 2000; Lumsden and Wilson 1981) and, in its general approach, evolutionary psychology (Barkow, Cosmides, and Tooby, 1992; Cosmides, Tooby, and Cronin 2001; Pinker 2002) seems to have something of the *déjà vu* about it—as though the century of development of theorizing in the specifically social and cultural (as opposed to behavioral-psychological) sciences, anthropology among them, had not occurred so as inevitably to change the terms of discourse for anyone who had been paying attention.

3. Note, too, how congenial here is recapitulationism of the "ontogeny recapitulates phylogeny" variety. In such recapitulationist views, children, "primitives," and various kinds of defectives manifest more elementary—that is, typologically prior—versions of the phenomena. Such "stadialist" views, when they convert typologies into theories of stages of development, need not, of course, be uniformitarian; they can be catastrophist, as in the sudden reorganization of a mentality (cf. Freud on psychosexual organization; Piaget on cognition; Kohlberg on moral sentiment) or a group's destiny (cf. Christian conversion; capitalism).

4. Note how we can understand the Boasian counterargument to social evolutionism in a biological evolutionary idiom. Boasian "cosmographic" historicism is the argument that most trait "analogies" are not, in fact, "homologies"—that is, traces of stages of history from a common ancestral sociocultural form in a unilinear and deterministic course of change. Hence, the characteristic study is the demonstration of different paths of diffusional cumulation of traits so as to form cultural "complexes" that might look superficially the same but have emerged in situ from very different histories even in geographically adjacent societies.

5. We recognize, of course, a hybrid and ultimately reductive type of self-styled "functionalism" in the Malinowskian tradition—culture as a "vast metaphor on digestion," as it was called. Here, the terms of comparison are not always "social facts" about normed practices and their place or contributory position to sustaining a society as such. Rather, "function" is a concept close to "needs requiring satisfaction" in which the individual human is the first matrix of "need," to the functional satisfaction of which social custom exists. Institutional forms become nodes of adjudication or rationalization of those various and sometimes competing needs, sometimes taking off with a "functional" life of their own. Malinowski himself, never a clear or consistent thinker in such matters (as compared, for example, with Radcliffe-Brown and his intellectual progeny), waffles on the degree to which "functions" are either directly or indirectly psychobiological in nature (recall the early controversy with Freud's apologist Ernest Jones; cf. Spiro 1982). Malinowskian "functionalism" was always closer to the hearts of American anthropologists who wanted to negotiate the terrain between the biological and the cultural, between the psychological and even psychiatric and the cultural. Hence the congeniality of Malinowskianism to certain culture-and-personality theorists in the 1930s, for example, who quickly abandoned the terrain of the

cosmographic Boasianism of, say, a Ruth Benedict. One thinks here of Mead, of Linton, and of various others around them.

6. Note as well its somewhat autonomous American counterpart in George Peter Murdock's *Social Structure* (1949), organized around functional principles of social morphology. This typological approach continues in the Human Relations Area Files, which has stimulated comparative study of group practices and values of cultures as so many traits dimensionalized into crosscutting domains. It should also be noted that Lévi-Strauss's *Les Structures élémentaires de la parenté* of the same year is a fully structural-functional work, albeit with a deeper generalizing analytic than anything Murdock imagined possible. (See also Lévi-Strauss's chapters on kinship in the two volumes of his *Structural Anthropology* 1958; 1973.)

7. In this connection, Meyer Fortes's "Time and Social Structure" (1970 [1949]) is a kind of culminative paper. It draws out at great analytic and statistical length the distinction between the contingent functional phases of a perduring structure of social arrangements and that social structure itself, in its unchanging "functional" contribution to a perduring social order. Functional phases are measurable over chronological time, though observing them might lead one—erroneously—to believe that practices have changed (rather than merely reflecting contingent rates of realization depending on phase and other system-exogenous factors). So there are two "times" or temporal dimensions that one must try to separate, only one of which is directly relevant to structural-functional typologies of social practices. From the perspective of this first order of "time," the second is merely the system synchronically working or "functioning" in its intersecting social-structural dimensions, with statistically measurable differences over the phases.

8. We should recall here that the "science (a.k.a. [social] evolution)" versus "history (a.k.a. humanities)" debate raged at its height in the 1930s between A. L. Kroeber, Boas's shockingly apostate first Columbia Ph.D., and the Master. See the series of exchanges on both sides reproduced in their respective *gesammelte Schriften* volumes, Kroeber (1952) on the side of superorganic and macrosociological "science" and Boas (1940b) on the side of cosmographic "history" that comprehends the individual-in-culture. Over the years there have been variant American excrescences of the first, such as Steward's (1955), Leslie White's (1987, 17–153), and Harris's (1968, 1979, 1999) strange brews of self-styled macrosociological "materialism," all in their own ways critical of Boas's reactive and "cosmographic" historical anti-evolutionism. And we should note that the culture and personality movement's embracing of a loosely Malinowskian functionalism (via its commitment to psychiatric Freudianism)—Mead and her circle, Kluckhohn, and others generationally junior—is a parallel search for status as science with a synchronicist program incorporable, in this case, into human psychobiology (cf. nn. 2, 3 above). But here "science" does not contrast with "history" so much as with the narrative and representational humanities, such as the ideal anthropology envisaged by Benedict (reprinted in Mead 1959, 459–470).

9. Surely Durkheim and Boas, exact coevals by birth, were already arguing these important points about the specificity and contrastive relativity of every

society's classification-inducing social practices and languages as central theses of their theoretical programs, in reaction to earlier formulations. Of course, a continuing trace of these traditions within anthropology can be seen in the "(sociocultural) relativity" versus "(universal) rationality" debates that spring up whenever sociocultural anthropologists confront one or another universalist discourse such as psychology, analytically inspired philosophical ethics, etc.

10. Literatures in both areas are, by now, immense, but one might consult the charmingly debunking *Aping Language*, by Joel Wallman (1992), on the first and John Lucy's crisply conceptualized accounts (1992, esp. 127–187; 1996, 1997) on the second).

11. Marshall Sahlins long ago (1976) pointed out the framework of analogies and conceptual leaps to which "sociobiology" of the time—freshly systematized in the first edition of E. O. Wilson's textbook/treatise (1975)—seemed to summon anthropological phenomena. Of course, perhaps the most famous example of this utility of anthropological data to arguments couched within the panspecific idiom of total reproductive fitness has been Napoleon Chagnon's (1968) now highly controversial descriptions of the Yanomamö of lowland Amazonia, the *"Fierce People"* in the *"Darkness"* of *"El Dorado"* (Tierney 2000).

12. See Leonard Bloomfield's (1933, 321–345) brilliant summary of this position in his classic treatise and the older references given there.

13. Of course, we must recognize that Lévi-Strauss's use of such a chemical calque/image has itself been mediated by Jakobson's earlier calque. In several works, Jakobson dubbed his distinctive feature analysis in phonology—which Lévi-Strauss cites as the exemplar in his "structural" writings—a "splitting" of the "atom of sound," the pointlike Saussurean phoneme, into its internal structure of component features. On the basis of the theory of features, the combinatoric typologies of both phonemic inventories and phonological syllables become possible. As is well known, Lévi-Strauss attended Jakobson's famous New York lectures of 1942, "Six leçons sur le son et le sens" [Six sessions on sound and sense], published in English translation—with a "preface" by Lévi-Strauss—only in 1978.

14. Within cognitive anthropology, in one of the earliest published papers on the "componential analysis" of kinship vocabularies, Floyd Lounsbury (1956, 191–192) gives an explicit tabular comparison between the phonemic versus phonetic perspective on analyzing sound systems and the semantic versus denotational perspective on analyzing meaning systems. (Huddleston 1974 deftly takes apart the calque underlying such work by Lounsbury, Goodenough, and others, showing how it leads to incoherence or triviality—or both—as an account of the reference-sense component of the meaningfulness of language.) Of course, by 1960 Kenneth Pike had generalized the distinction in phonemics/phonology into the famous—and famously misunderstood!—"emic" versus "etic" one. He was emphasizing the applicability of this distinction to all meaningful aspects of culture, no less than to language in its denoting lexicon, in his *Language in Relation to a Unified Theory of the Structure of Human Behavior* (1967 [1954–1960]).

15. As post–World War II phonologists and communications engineers dis-

cussed channel capacities and related matters in terms of "digital" (binary) and "analogue" coding principles, early students of what developed into cognitive psychology and contemporary cognitive science began to glimpse anew the importance of the categorical functional principles so clearly exemplified in the diverse sound systems of the world's languages—for example, G. Miller (1951); Bruner, Goodnow, and Austin (1956); Brown (1958)—from the era of a mutually fructifying discourse among information theory, linguistics, and psychology. The ubiquitous integrating figure of Roman Jakobson looms large in this discourse after his postwar renaissance in the United States, first at Columbia and then, especially, at Harvard-MIT.

16. Joseph Greenberg (1966, 100–111) elaborates the significance of such "universals of kinship terminological systems" in terms of a theory of asymmetric lexical coding of certain genealogically based distinctions, the "markedness" of lexicalization. The regularities can be stated like any other "implicational universals" of language: informally, for any E[go], if a language L codes egocentric genealogical position $g_n(E)$ with a simple lexical form ("my [noun]"), then it codes position $g_{n-1}(E)$ with that same lexical form along particular, regularly computable genealogical chains in which $g_0(E) = E$ (specifically lexicalized coding is opposed to coding $g_{n-1}(E)$ with an iterated grammatical possessive construction, of the type exemplified in English, A's B's [. . .'s] Z). These chains connected by the criterion of being coded by the same simple lexical form define the dimensions of *possible* grouping of genealogical positions around a fixed ego E by simple lexical forms that anthropologists have long been seeking in studying kinterminologies. (See Lounsbury 1969a [1964], where it is called the method of "extensional" analysis.) In short, it provides a dimensionalized space within which we can comparatively locate all such terminological systems as occur or—if the hypothesis is correct—can occur. One's ability so to do establishes egocentrically reckoned genealogy as a central *denotational domain* of the lexical forms called "kinterms" insofar as it has predictive power with respect to some area of lexicon of any language whatsoever. Note it does not say that such terms are exclusively used for egocentrically reckoned genealogical denotata (we know that this is not the case, especially in so-called "address" usage); nor that such denotation exhaustively characterizes the total meaningfulness of such linguistic forms when they occur as words in context; nor even that other simple lexical items in a given language, structured along nongenealogical principles of asymmetric coding, might not be part of an overall lexicon of dyadic (or even n-adic) terms of inherently relational status, of which kin relations are always a paradigmatic or focal set. Greenberg's straightforward—and correct—clarification of the matter in structural-linguistic terms conformable to Jakobsonian "markedness" theory in linguistics seems, however, not to have influenced either self-styled "componential analysts" or their opponents such as David Schneider. Greenberg, let us note, rightly points back to Kroeber's classic 1909 paper as having more or less founded the field of comparative kinterminological lexicography in (egocentric) genealogical domains.

17. Among "emicizing" theorists, Goodenough (1970), almost uniquely, does

make clear that such comparative perspective is immanent in—that is, dialectically presupposed by—any description of a phenomenon of "*a* culture." Unfortunately, he seems to view "culture" as a cognitive system of knowledge focused on categories, the very evidence for which is comprised of denotational use of lexical forms. So not much of "culture" beyond lexicon can, in point of fact, be addressed in this way.

18. Focal sites for the eruption of institutional strife precisely along such battle lines have been university departments of anthropology, which have in several instances fissioned along subdisciplinary lines, and organizational programs and activities like meetings and journals, as within the American Anthropological Association and its constituent groupings. Interestingly, given the last century's history of the field, as noted above, the essentializing rallying cry of at least one side continues to be "Science" versus whatever those other guys [or gays? or gals?] are doing.

19. To be sure, there had long been a minority undertow in British social anthropology, represented by such figures as A. M. Hocart and especially the later Evans-Pritchard, who came to realize that cultural phenomena required a comparative, hermeneutic, and historical science (cf. Boas's "cosmography"). But such writers had little impact on the main currents of anthropological theorizing of the sort I have been describing.

20. The cover term "symbolic anthropology" is intended to include several theoretical lines of descent. One was from David Schneider, who spoke explicitly of "symbols and meanings." Another was from Victor Turner, who moved beyond a Mancunian structural-functionalism to what he called anthropology as "comparative symbology," grounded principally in what, in more semiotically informed discourse, we term iconism and its role in social imagining and social process. (Cf. here also the influential work of Nancy Munn.) And yet a third was from Clifford Geertz, who, moving beyond such iconism as characterized his earlier work, has emphasized the self-presentation of culture to both "natives" and anthropologists as public "ensembles of texts" requiring interpretation by a hermeneutic science. (Unfortunately, Geertz willy-nilly imports from Ricoeur and others an unrethought notion of the "text," making this theoretical outlook highly problematic in a number of ways. See Silverstein and Urban 1996.)

21. Surely this is the important larger theoretical point, beyond the historical specifics of the various cases, suggested some years back by the insights of "the invention of tradition" work among historians reported in Hobsbawm and Ranger (1983). Ceremonials, aesthetic creations, and other such phenomena are sites par excellence for at once invoking and creating "culture" and "language"; though a truism, anthropologists needed this reminder of the high degree of historical and sociological specificity of "timeless" culture.

22. I believe Sahlins (2000c [1993]) early pointed out the irony that "natives" now all want to be recognized for their very own "language" and "culture" just as many anthropologists proclaim local "languages" and "cultures" to be dead in the face of "globalization" and "cultural flows." As well, Sahlins thereby points out certain parallels of process today to what is now termed the European Renais-

sance and the rise of ethnonational consciousness. Appadurai (1996) as well sees the fact that there is effort—the "work" of "culture"—involved for social groups in achieving some equilibrium state of group-centered "locality," for a language and a culture as consciousness must redefine itself within the framing reach of such larger-scale forces. See my development of this concept for "local" language communities in Silverstein (1998) and references there on the local constructivity of the cultural concept of "language."

23. A huge scholarly and applied field, frequently termed "language endangerment," has developed within linguistics. It merges Boasian concern for "obsolescent languages" (Swadesh 1948) in the pressured social conditions of "language death" observed especially by salvage ethnographers and linguists; structural and sociolinguistic studies of the varied competences of language users in such situations (e.g., Dorian 1973, 1981; cf. Dorian 1989); and an applied linguistics program in respect of such language communities, focusing on documentation and archiving, stabilization through the sociocultural paraphernalia of standardization, heritage language pedagogy, etc. (Fishman 1991, 2001; Hinton and Hale 2001; Hill et al. 2002).

24. See, for example, Silverstein (1972, 1996, 1997), focusing on North American material. Several textbooks on pidgin and creole languages now exist—for example, in Holm (1988–1989); Mühlhäusler (1986); Romaine (1988)—and there are several collections of sketches of these kinds of languages—for example, Thomason (1997)—and interpretative collections on the nature of pidginization, creolization, and decreolization—for example, Hymes (1971); Valdman (1977); Spears and Winford (1997).

25. The case of Michif, spoken in North Dakota and Manitoba by mixed-heritage descendants ultimately of Cree-speaking women and Canadian French—speaking *coureurs de bois* is particularly interesting, since features of both Algonquian grammar and French grammar are found, almost neatly split between verbs and their associated machinery and nouns and theirs! See Bakker (1997) and references there. During the nineteenth century, the question of whether or not "mixed languages" existed—English was suspected of being an example, note!— was very widely discussed; see William Dwight Whitney's (1971 [1882], 170–191) contribution, for example. Hugo Schuchardt, the famous student of pidgin, creole, and similar linguistic states, propounded a whole theory of mixed language as a challenge to the taxonomy-driven theories of neat divergent change. The great Prince Troubetzkoy, Jakobson's Prague School collaborator, later speculated that the vaunted Indo-European "parent language" itself was produced by language convergence and mixture. Reflexive discourses of one's own hybridity are local cultural forms of these beliefs—cf. for example the particular cultural form of "disemia" and "diglossia" described by Herzfeld (1987) for Greeks' thoughts about their cultural forms and language.

26. Three recent collections from linguistic anthropologists speak to these issues: Schieffelin, Woolard, and Kroskrity (1998); Kroskrity (2000); and Gal and Woolard (2001).

An Archaeology of the Four-Field Approach in Anthropology in the United States

IAN HODDER

My dominant reaction to the question of the four-field approach in anthropology in the United States is "Why only four fields?" A related question is "Why should I as an archaeologist accept anthropology as an umbrella discipline or as a metadiscourse?"

Of course, my response to this issue is as an archaeologist trained in Britain and Europe, where archaeology is more closely tied to history. By this I mean that most archaeology departments in Europe are not in anthropology or ethnography departments. Rather, they are within departments or schools of history or classics or Oriental studies. The training of students and their backgrounds are commonly in the arts and humanities rather than in the social sciences. In many cases, independent archaeology departments teach their own degrees without a larger umbrella (such as anthropology). It was David Clarke, a British theoretical archaeologist and prehistorian, who argued that "archaeology is archaeology is archaeology" (1968), and such a view of an independent discipline is taken for granted by many in Britain and Europe. The institutional ties of independent archaeology departments and museums are often with history in some form (although not universally; in Cambridge University archaeology is situated within a Faculty of Archaeology and Anthropology).

The location of archaeology within anthropology in the United States is itself historically contingent, as much as is the location of archaeology close to history and classics in Europe. The historical conditions that led to the varied alignments of disciplines in different parts of the world include both the internal developments of the disciplines and their alliances and the wider political context. The global development of different types of archaeology within different regional traditions as part of historical, social, and political differences has now been well documented (e.g., Trigger 1984, 1989; Cleere 1989; Ucko 1995). In Europe, the growth of archaeology is tied historically and politically with the project of the nation-state. The political vision and ambitions of the emerging nation-states provided the context for the first major museums and state antiquities authorities throughout Europe, and in relation to these developments academic archaeology came of age (the first professorships of archaeology or prehistory) in the nineteenth century (Daniel 1962). There were of course also colonial interests that stocked the major museums, but the primary concern of the new institutions dealing with the past was to define the antiquity and historical depth of the nation-state. In the United States, on the other hand, the initial influences on the development of archaeological institutions were more closely tied to colonialism within North America (Trigger 1984). The early impetus and the early institutions of archaeology were tied to defining the Native American "other." Archaeology was thus immediately linked to anthropology, and indeed the early debates, such as that surrounding the Moundbuilders, served to reinforce an anthropological rather than a historical perspective (Willey and Phillips 1958). As a long-term result of these differences between Europe and the United States, in Europe archaeology has a self-sufficient status linked to history and to the invention of national tradition. In the United States, the relationship with the precolonial past is more complex and is made relevant through anthropology.

Anthropology and Processual Archaeology

In the second half of the twentieth century, archaeology in the United States came further to embrace the mantle of anthropology and make a virtue of it. The American New Archaeology of the 1960s and early 1970s was much indebted to Leslie White and to the social-evolutionary theories of Sahlins, Service, and Fried (Binford 1962; Willey and Phillips 1958; Trigger 1989). Early studies in this new, self-consciously positivistic mode aped anthropology in a very direct sense. For example, a work entitled *Archaeology as Anthropology* attempted to discern postmarital residence rules from ceramic style distributions on sites (Longacre 1970), and Binford (1971) tried to argue that social variation could be read directly from burial variation. It became taken for granted that "Archaeology is anthropology, or it is nothing" (a claim made by a number of authors, including Binford 1962 and Willey and Phillips 1958).

The image of archaeology that was promoted within such research was as a subset of anthropology defined as a universalizing science using cross-cultural generalization. As the New Archaeology developed into a more mature processual archaeology in the 1970s and 1980s, some specific archaeological issues began to emerge; in particular there was recognition of the importance of depositional and postdepositional processes in the formation of the archaeological record (Schiffer 1976). But even as a more distinctly archaeological discourse emerged, the affiliation with anthropology was not doubted. There are those in archaeology in the United States—particularly selectionist and behavioral archaeologists—who still hold to some vision of a cross-cultural anthropological processual science as a basis for archaeology (Dunnell 1980; Schiffer 1999, 2000). Indeed it is probably still the case that most archaeologists in the United States retain some version of this vision. My comments are thus highly idiosyncratic in this U.S. context, since I do not take for granted such universalizing aims and I have not been part of a tradition in which anthropology has some form of natural right to define archaeology.

There is today an emergent and different historical context in which both anthropology and archaeology find themselves: postcolonialism, globalism, and the new forces of plurality and reflexivity (Hodder 1999). As cultural anthropology moved into a period of critique and into the linguistic and reflexive turns that have characterized debates over recent decades, most archaeologists in the United States seem to have clung to their unproblematic conception of archaeology and anthropology as positivistic sciences. For many in archaeology (e.g., Binford 1989), these moves in cultural anthropology were seen as a betrayal of anthropology from its true basis in science and the universal. The end result has been that processual archaeologists have seen themselves increasingly divorced from much cultural anthropology. Today there are several branches of processual archaeology that hold to the natural science image of the discipline, to positivism, and to the anthropological label. These approaches claim a "scientific archaeology." They include cognitive processual, behavioral, and selectionist views (Hodder 2001).

This retention of a processualist agenda in archaeology as it is found in the United States is important in the context of the debate about the four-field approach. The behavioralists, for example, reject much of socio-cultural anthropology, especially those parts that might be tinged with postmodernism, or even those concerned with meaning, agency, or dis-course. The distance between some archaeology and sociocultural an-thropology often seems great. For example, recently Schiffer, a behav-ioralist, noted that in his new book "readers may be nonplussed at the absence in the new theory of much vocabulary . . . such as meaning, sign, symbol, intention, motivation, purpose, goal, attitude, value, belief, norm, function, mind, and culture. Despite Herculean efforts in the social sciences to define these often ethnocentric or metaphysical notions, they remain behaviorally problematic and so are superfluous in the present project" (1999, 9). The gap here between behavioral archaeology and anthropology appears cavernous. Behavioral and processual archaeolo-gists often counter that the gap between archaeology (as they conceive it) and anthropology has emerged because sociocultural anthropology has, in effect, abandoned being anthropological. If only sociocultural anthro-pology could abandon its turn to history and language, they argue, the gap would be closed. As it stands, however, most of sociocultural anthro-pology seems devoid of interest for Schiffer. Given such views and di-vergences of opinion, it seems unhelpful to continue to pretend that ar-chaeology (as defined by Schiffer and many processual archaeologists) is anthropology, or indeed that it has anything to do with anthropology at all as it is widely practiced today.

It seems to me that similar tensions between archaeology and socio-cultural anthropology abound in the United States; there seems to be a real fault line that is thinly held together by tradition, training, placement issues, etc. It seems to me much healthier if in such contexts the arbitrari-ness of the historical connection between archaeology and anthropology is admitted and the disciplines, or parts of them, go their own ways and forge new alliances.

There are many ways in which one might argue for harm done by the location of archaeology within anthropology in the United States. Some of the problems concern the restraint in such a context on the devel-opment of debates with other disciplines, such as between archaeology and history (achieved more effectively in historical archaeology; Morris 2000). But also the development of archaeological science has been im-peded. I refer here to the numerous techniques and skills described as archaeometry. There appear to be few graduate programs in archaeological science in the United States in anthropology departments. It is common, if not usual, for these to exist as master's programs in the United Kingdom and Europe, and in my view this is a very important development. The use of scientific techniques in archaeology (such as X-ray diffraction, scanning electron microscopy, micromorphology, the analysis of ancient DNA, etc.) depends in my view on the training of researchers competent in both the techniques and the problems to which they can be applied. I am sure that the reasons for the paucity of such training in anthropology programs in the United States are complex, but the location of archaeology with cultural anthropology in academic departments and within social and behavioral funding agencies may be relevant.

Also in the United States there seems to have been an unhelpful confusion between scientific archaeology and archaeological science. In Britain "archaeological science" is equated with the use of scientific techniques, regardless of theoretical or epistemological persuasion. It is not a partisan or loaded term. In the United States, "archaeological science" seems more closely linked to an overarching model of a scientific archaeology, defined in positivistic terms. People thus often seem surprised that I, while rejecting a positivistic scientific archaeology, use so many natural science techniques. This confusion between techniques and their mode of employment has perhaps inhibited a proper funding of archaeological science within departments dominated by cultural anthropology.

Where archaeological science has been able to be fully developed, it certainly takes archaeology beyond the four fields. Take, for example, the case of Martin Jones's *Molecule Hunt: Archaeology and the Search for Ancient DNA* (2001). The impact of the new genetic technologies and the debates surrounding ancient DNA analysis have been very far-reaching in archaeology (see also Renfrew 2000). A whole array of new problems and questions has opened up. While these issues may have an anthropological dimension, particularly with reference to biological anthropology, they also involve archaeologists directly with biologists. Similarly, the ability to study lipid residues in ceramics has been most effective when involving direct connections to biochemists (e.g., Copley, Clark, and Evershed 2004). It seems that some parts of archaeology would be better served either by separating from anthropology or by aligning themselves to the natural sciences, biology, human genetics, the behavioral sciences, and so on.

I have not mentioned a further important factor that has tended to pull processual archaeology in the United States away from anthropology. The development of contract archaeology (cultural resource management) was based on the definition of the material remains of the past as a "resource" to be managed following government guidelines and least-cost principles. The professionalization of archaeology that resulted involved the establishment of professional bodies and systems of training that focused less on anthropological questions and more on technical skills. A tension often emerged between field practitioners and "anthropological archaeologists." Many professional field archaeologists have come to feel that they were not properly trained to be archaeologists within anthropology departments in universities. For some archaeologists at least it seems clear, given these professional needs, that it is in archaeology's best interests to forge disciplinary relationships that are unfettered by the four-field scheme.

Postprocessual Approaches

In addition to the various types of processual archaeologies, there is a bewildering variety of postprocessual views in archaeology, including feminist, phenomenological, dialectical, and hermeneutic approaches. *Postprocessual archaeology* is a term that emerged in Britain in the 1980s as a reaction against processual archaeology (Johnson 1999; Whitley 1998). In many ways, it was just "post." In other words, rather than having a unified agenda, it was based on critique and on exploring a diversity of positions that countered the tenets of processual archaeology. Put together with the diversity that also emerged within processual approaches, archaeology suddenly became very diverse in the late 1980s and 1990s.

While I think that many archaeologists, including many in the United States, would agree that archaeology is more internally divided than it has ever been, some processualists would decry this situation and would argue for a need to restore order and unity. They contrast the "one science" model of positivist processual archaeology with the dangerous postmodern tendencies of cultural anthropology and postprocessual archaeology. For example, Schiffer fears that archaeology might become like sociocultural anthropology with no "common ground, no core set of concepts and principles. . . . I hoped that we could, at all costs, avoid that unpleasant outcome" (2000, vii–viii) My own view is that this diversity is beneficial for the discipline; it creates dynamism and pushes research forward. I feel fortified in this view by work in other disciplines, such as the studies by Galison of physics. Galison (1997) sees physics as divided into multiple cultures that engage in a trading zone of competing ideas and approaches. The "whole" of physics is actually an unstable but productive compromise among groups with different assumptions, methods, and aims. Archaeology as a discipline is both more mature and more fragmented than it was, with many kaleidoscopes of variation. The variation in archaeology today extends across a wide spectrum, and many volumes have appeared recently trying to capture this diversity in theory and method (e.g., Ucko 1995; Whitley 1998; J. Thomas 2001).

Although postprocessual archaeology can be seen to encompass a wide diversity of positions, many were and are held together by a critique of the positivism of processual archaeology, by an embrace of history and agency, and by an engagement with meaning and practice. Other terms, such as *interpretive archaeology*, have been used (e.g., J. Thomas 2001; Tilley 1993) in order to capture a degree of coherence and direction. In defining the new coherence, most postprocessual archaeologists have forged close links to the social sciences, including anthropology. For example, the early emphasis on the notion that material culture is meaningfully constituted owed a considerable debt to Turner, Lévi-Strauss, Douglas, Geertz, Sahlins, and others (Johnson 1999; Hodder 1986). The postprocessual focus on history was as much indebted to anthropologists such as Sahlins (1981) as it was to historians such as Collingwood and Braudel (Bintliff 1991; Knapp 1992). Many postprocessual approaches to power, critique, and phenomenology (e.g., D. Miller and Tilley 1984; J. Thomas 2001) were primarily directly influenced by sources outside anthropology such as Giddens, Foucault, Derrida, and Heidegger, but there was often still a "looking over one's shoulder" at cultural anthropology to see how translations and applications of the ideas had been made in a related discipline (e.g., in Tilley's 1996 *Ethnography of the Neolithic*).

Another important area of postprocessual archaeology that draws it closer to contemporary debates in cultural anthropology is the focus on the intersections between heritage and globalization. In turning toward an archaeology embedded within social life, archaeologists became concerned with the politics of the past, and in this they joined debates within museums and heritage (Merriman 1991; Lowenthal 1985; Fowler 1992). Part of the debate regarding the role of the past in the present concerns the impact of various forces on the link between the past and the nation-state. Various international agencies (from UNESCO and the European Union to the World Bank and conservation NGOs) now have the ability to insert themselves between the nation-state and "its" past. At the same time, the proliferation of cultural tourism and the commercialization of the material past and archaeological monuments have become major factors in the management of heritage. In the debate of such developments, critical approaches in archaeology have developed a complex literature that deals with issues such as identity, locality, authenticity, diaspora, and transnationalism—themes that intersect with debates in cultural anthropology (Meskell 2002; Clifford 1997a; Appadurai 1996).

Other postprocessual archaeologists have embraced the reflexive turns in the social sciences. In my view the influences here were not primarily from anthropology, though writers such as Clifford played a part. Rather, the main influences were from French philosophy and linguistics (Derrida—see Bapty and Yates 1990; Foucault—see D. Miller and Tilley 1984 and Shanks and Tilley 1987); sociology (Bryan Turner and Giddens—see Parker Pearson 1982); and feminism (Gero and Conkey 1991). These reflexive moves have led to experiments with new forms of writing and presentation of the past (e.g., Joyce 2002; Pearson and Sullivan 1999) and the use of new media (Tringham 1994). They have also led to new approaches to "fieldwork"—the location of excavation and field survey within a critical and reflexive perspective (Andrews, Barrett, and Lewis 2000; Hodder 1999; Yarrow 2003). These new developments of archaeological fieldwork parallel debates in ethnography (Marcus and Fischer 1986; Clifford and Marcus 1986; Gupta and Ferguson 1997). Perhaps the major impetus to reflexive methods in archaeology has come not solely from theory, but also from the interactions between archaeologists and indigenous groups taking back control of their rights to the past (Watkins 2000). The impact of the Native American Graves Protection and Repatriation Act (NAGPRA) in the United States has been considerable, but in other parts of the world productive interactions with archaeologists have led to collaborative and reflexive research (Anyon et al. 2000; Smith et al. 1995). In these ways, developments in postprocessual archaeology parallel the debates about reflexivity in cultural anthropology (Lynch 2000; Salzman 2002).

As an example of the increased alliances between postprocessual archaeology and mainstream social-cultural anthropology in the United

States, I would like to refer to my own experience. I have never taken an anthropological course (by which I mean a course taught in an anthropology department) in my life (though I have taught many), and I do not see myself as an "anthropologist" as that term is defined by many archaeologists in the United States. And yet I feel very much at home in the Department of Social and Cultural Anthropology at Stanford, where I now teach. In fact I feel much more at home there than I would in most archaeology departments. Why is this? Sun, sail, and cocktails certainly help, but the main reason is undoubtedly that we read the same books and have the same theoretical and methodological interests, even though we supposedly are in different disciplines. On the whole, I feel that we can talk to each other better and that we have more in common than I do with an archaeologist who is a selectionist or behaviorist or hard-line processualist. The starting assumptions are the same, whereas everything is alien when I talk to my non-postprocessual colleagues in archaeology. I have a similar experience when in a psychology seminar on agency or in a geography seminar on landscape: there is a commonality of major texts and orientation. Of course, archaeologists of different theoretical persuasions may share a familiarity with certain types of data or fieldwork experience, but these ties do not necessarily provide a foundation for an intellectual sharing of ideas and for productive dialogue and support.

I have been arguing that postprocessual archaeology is closer to mainstream cultural anthropology than are other types of archaeology at present. An example of this coming together is seen in the new *Journal of Social Archaeology*, which aims to cover themes with broad interest in the social sciences. For example, its first issue included an interview with Arjun Appadurai, and its editorial board has archaeologists but includes many others such as Judith Butler, Sherry Ortner, Bryan Turner, and Sylvia Yanagisako. There are perhaps many reasons why such authors from a range of human sciences should be willing to be associated with archaeology. At least one reason might be the widespread fascination in the human and social sciences with the metaphor of archaeology. The idea of carrying out "an archaeology" of contemporary discourses, institutions, cultural traits, and so on has different resonances in different contexts. But the widespread use of the metaphor suggests that an archaeology of anthropology might be feasible—and thus that archaeology could provide a metadiscourse for anthropology rather than the other way around.

Toward an Archaeological Anthropology

If we invert the processual archaeological emphasis on an anthropological archaeology, what might an archaeological anthropology look like, beyond the metaphorical Foucauldian "archaeology of . . ." approach? In my view, such a development would involve two main components: materiality and the long term. One impetus toward an archaeological approach to anthropological questions stems from practice theories and histories of technology studies. Archaeologists are skilled at focusing on the practices of daily life, and they readily integrated Bourdieu (1977) and other approaches dealing with the mundane and the everyday (De Certeau 1984; Barrett 1994). Studies of the history of contemporary technologies have also been influential in showing the importance of material-social links. There has also been a convergence of interests and a unifying of literature around the theme of material culture (D. Miller 1987; Tilley 1999). At University College, London, there is even a subdepartment of material culture that includes both archaeologists and anthropologists. The *Journal of Material Culture* contains many examples of "archaeological" approaches within ethnographic studies. Recent studies of contemporary material culture (e.g., Buchli and Lucas 2001) contribute excavation and material culture methods to issues of social change among contemporary groups. While at one level such studies simply extend from historical archaeological analysis of the recent past (Voss and Schmidt 2000), at another level they offer a new dimension of study—"the archaeology of us" (Rathje 1979). Examples include the excavation and analysis of refuse left by squatters in order to identify aspects of lifestyle that are not available from observation of living contexts, verbal questionnaires, and surveys (Buchli and Lucas 2001). In another example, Buchli (1999) has studied the architecture and daily practices within the Narkomfin apartment bloc in Moscow in order to explore how people responded to and worked within changing state practices in twentieth-century Russia. It could be argued, therefore, that a dimension of the training of cultural anthropology students could deal with approaches to the analysis of material culture—to study what is expressed in the nondiscursive practices of daily life. This would involve methods familiar to archaeologists, such as the planning of what is left behind, the recording of layers and relationships, the typological description of artifacts, the study of use and wear, and the analysis of residues.

The work of Bruno Latour (e.g., 1993) has been the most influential in pushing archaeologists toward a more radical conception of materiality. Here the focus is on breaking down any trace of an opposition between subject and object. In Latour's writings, objects become humans, endowed with agency (see also Haraway 1991). In archaeology (e.g., Olsen 2003), the challenge is to explore the way in which technologies and material engagements are seamlessly material and social, to examine how material entanglements (N. Thomas 1991) have social dimensions. Some of the most detailed studies of material affordances derive from the French school of technology studies (e.g., Lemonnier 1986; Dobres 2000) and also from behavioral archaeology (e.g., Schiffer 1999, 2000). In the archaeological training of cultural anthropologists, the value of such archaeological approaches to social life is to increase sensitivity to the ways in which what appears on the surface as a social interaction may be embedded in and laced with material properties. It is in the material act that the seamless coming together of different aspects of life occurs.

Another possible strut of an archaeological anthropology, the long term, is less developed. Cultural anthropology has of course had its "historical turn," as in the work of Sahlins (1981). There has already been much collaboration between archaeologists and anthropologists in terms of the creation of historical perspectives on contemporary groups (e.g., Kirch and Sahlins 1992). Archaeology and ethnography have worked closely together in researching the development of central Asian nomadism (Evans and Humphrey 2003), or in exploring the forms of metallurgy in southern and eastern Africa (Schmidt 1997), or in understanding social variation in Madagascar (Parker Pearson 2002). Historians, ethnohistorians, ethnographers, and archaeologists have been involved in the debates about the evolutionary status and history of hunter-gatherers in southern Africa (e.g., Wilmsen 1989; Dowson and Lewis-Williams 1994; Huffman 1984). Perhaps the greatest claim for the dependence of contemporary geopolitics on the distant past is made by Diamond (1997) or by Renfrew (1987). But by referring to the long term, I wish to draw attention to scales of analysis that go beyond an archaeological approach to the history of contemporary societies. Beyond the "historical turn," I would point toward an "archaeological turn," in which the study of the long term is linked to approaches regarding materiality and nondiscursive practice.

The aim here would be to explore how entanglements with objects over the long term lie behind visible and discursive social changes. Historians such as Elias (1994 [1936]) have been effective in showing how minor changes in manners and "appropriate behavior" can set the stage for large-scale social and economic change. In archaeology, Johnson (1996) has shown how the "rise of capitalism" can be seen as embedded within very long-term shifts in notions of privacy, ownership, and property. Such approaches attempt to avoid uncritical assumptions about essentialized traditions or "indigenous" continuities. Rather, they explore what one might call "scalarity," the way in which dimensions of a daily act observed by an ethnographer intersect with temporal scales of action of which no individual actor can be cognizant. A full "archaeological" approach to such issues would explore how various types of entanglement with the material world lead to long-term entailments (Hamann 2002; Bradley 1993; Lechtman 1996).

Beyond materiality and the long term, there is another way in which an archaeological anthropology might be conceived. This additional perspective grows out of the collaborative field research identified above. In some cases, anthropologists and ethnographers have attempted to understand the social construction of archaeological knowledge (e.g., Abu El-Haj 2001), or they have contributed to the interaction between archaeologists and local and other stakeholder communities on archaeological field projects or surveys (Bartu 2000). Such work involves an "archaeological" anthropology in that it is an anthropology designed to contribute to archaeology in one way or another. In my own field project at Çatalhöyük in central Turkey, an important aim has been to involve local communities and other stakeholder groups in the construction of knowledge about the site. The local communities are not essentialized as "close to the past" but are simply seen as stakeholders that can contribute from a particular perspective—one of many (Hodder 1999). But the interactions with the different communities that have an interest in the site involve many levels of complexity. To fully understand the impact of the excavation of the site on these communities involves in-depth and sensitive, time-consuming analysis and interpretation. Archaeologists have long been used to "working with the locals," and they have long and increasingly been involved in collaborative projects, as outlined above. But if such interactions are to be taken seriously, they merit careful study and detailed engagement. This is why at Çatalhöyük, a number of ethnographers have been involved—especially Ayfer Bartu (2000) and David Shankland (1996).

In my view, then, archaeological projects benefit from the inclusion of ethnographers who work alongside the excavation or field project exploring the complexities of the interactions with communities and trying to promote dialogue and collaboration. Such anthropologists or ethnographers have to be "archaeological" in the sense that their training requires a full understanding of the ways in which archaeological fieldwork is conducted. An alternative view is that a new type of cultural anthropology/archaeology student can be trained to have equal dexterity and competence in both archaeology and ethnography. Whatever the specific solution, a close link in the training of archaeology and cultural anthropology students is again required.

Does this emphasis on an "archaeological anthropology" herald a return to the four fields? I think not. We are not seeing here an overall rapprochement between archaeology and anthropology (Gosden 1999; Orme 1981). I have tried to show that only some segments of archaeological research, theory, and method are engaged in activities that lead toward a close interaction between the disciplines. Many archaeologists have very different interests, which take them toward history or the natural sciences. Most archaeologists spend most of their time dealing with environmental mitigation, planning processes, and contracting firms. Many of the major influences on the archaeological study of materiality and the long term stem from sociology, philosophy, technology studies, and so on as much as from anthropology. What is of note is that a productive link between archaeology and anthropology emerges only in a limited space. At a particular contingent moment, there is the desire for interaction. What is also of note is that potential for interaction is greatest where the two disciplines are sovereign and bring their own expertise and questions to the table. This is not an image of four fields locked into a common set of interests, but of independent disciplines coming together strategically to deal with specific issues. Nor is this an image of a dominant field "anthropology" in which various subfields are made to nestle. Rather it is an image of quite separate fields, with different areas of expertise and different methods, coming to the table as equals. At other times, they sit at quite other tables, with quite different disciplines, ranging from the humanities (especially history) to the natural sciences.

Integration Beyond the Four Fields

One can then develop a vision of anthropology, archaeology, and the social sciences in which groups of coworkers come together around themes and perspectives such as social agency and meaning, materiality, genetics, language, or selectionism. In each group the alliances are in different directions, and they extend out to include researchers outside the traditional four fields, such as those in history, psychology, cultural studies, or biology. In such a context there is no need for a metadiscourse provided by anthropology or by any other one discipline. Rather, strategic alliances can be made with biology, psychology, art history, or classics. But in each case the alliance is founded on area studies (such as Near Eastern studies) or themes and topics such as selectionism, behaviorism, phenomenology, and feminism. This would allow people of like mind and like interest to engage with each other in fruitful ways and without the constraints of "big brother" anthropology.

The danger of creating alliances of this type might be that students trained within one of these areas, themes, or topics would end up narrow and unaware of the full range of argument across the human sciences. However, it can be argued that it is a characteristic of undergraduate courses across many disciplines today that they are forced to cover an overly narrow range. The widely used method of distribution requirements can be used to achieve greater flexibility among related disciplines and topic and area studies programs at the undergraduate level. This structure would produce graduates accustomed to moving more flexibly and finding specializations that crosscut traditional four-field categorizations. It might be argued that the prescription being proposed here for archaeology—flexible alliances around an independent core—is of relevance only to archaeology and that other disciplines are best served by clear boundaries and well-defined disciplinary knowledge. In fact, it seems that many universities struggle much of the time with the widespread issue of how to crosscut among departments, research themes, and area studies. Archaeology is not special in this way. The prescription of flexible alliances can be applied in many, if not all, areas of research.

There are clearly many strains in the current relationship between archaeology and anthropology in the United States. While the individual disciplines of the four fields may continue to provide a useful framework for teaching, advanced teaching and research have already moved in directions characterized by fragmentation and the formation of new interdisciplinary alliances beyond the boundaries of the four fields. In this more complex, open, and fluid world of ever-changing intellectual alliances, the major challenges are organizational and infrastructural. How is it possible to preserve some semblance of disciplinarity while at the same time allowing for changing allegiances and changing interest groups? Apart from its nostalgic value, the four-field scheme offers only restrictions in such a context.

It remains important to grasp opportunities for revised systems of training when and where close ties are developed among areas of the social sciences. In the example discussed here of the close relationships between postprocessual archaeology and various aspects of cultural anthropology, there is a need and an opportunity to train cultural anthropology students in the recording of material practice, long-term material entailments, and the relationships between archaeological knowledge construction and stakeholder communities. At the same time, archaeology students would benefit from training in reflexive methods, globalization, and historical anthropology. In these more limited and specific ways, independent and separate disciplines collaborate and learn from each other.

NOTE

I would like to thank the editors and reviewers for their comments on an earlier version of this essay.

REFERENCES

Aarsleff, Hans. 1982. *From Locke to Saussure: Essays on the Study of Language and Intellectual History.* Minneapolis: University of Minnesota Press.

Abu El-Haj, Nadia. 2001. *Facts on the Ground: Archaeological Practice and Territorial Self-Fashioning in Israeli Society.* Chicago: University of Chicago Press.

Adams, William. 1998. *The Philosophical Roots of Anthropology.* Stanford: CSLI Publications.

American Anthropological Association. 2004. Website at *www.aaanet.org.*

Andrews, G., J. Barrett, and J. Lewis. 2000. "Interpretation Not Record: The Practice of Archaeology." *Antiquity* 74: 525–530.

Anthropology News. 2003 "Media Monitor." *Anthropology News* 44 (4): 25.

Anyon, R., T. J. Ferguson, L. Jackson, and L. Lane. 1996. "Native eAmerican Oral Traditions and Archaeology." *Society for American Archaeology Bulletin* 14, no. 2: 14–16.

Appadurai, Arjun. 1996. *Modernity at Large: Cultural Dimensions of Globalization.* Minneapolis: University of Minnesota Press.

Asad, Talal, ed. 1973. *Anthropology and the Colonial Encounter.* New York: Humanities Press.

Baker, Lee. 1998. *From Savage to Negro: Anthropology of and Construction of Race, 1896–1954.* Berkeley: University of California Press.

Bakker, Peter. 1997. *A Language of Our Own: The Genesis of Michif, the Mixed Cree-French Language of the Canadian Métis.* New York: Oxford University Press.

Bapty, Ian, and Timothy Yates. 1990. *Archaeology after Structuralism.* London: Routledge.

Barkow, Jerome H., Leda Cosmides, and John Tooby, eds. 1992. *The Adapted Mind: Evolutionary Psychology and the Generation of Culture.* New York: Oxford University Press.

Barnes, R. H. 1987. "Anthropological Comparison." In *Comparative Anthropology.* Ed. L. Holy. New York: Blackwell.

Barrett, John. 1994. *Fragments from Antiquity: An Archaeology of Social Life in Britain, 2900–1200 B. C.* Oxford: Blackwell.

Barth, Fredrik, ed. 1969. *Ethnic Groups and Boundaries: The Social Organization of Cultural Difference.* Boston: Little Brown.

Bartu, Ayfer. 2000. "Working with Local Communities." In *Towards Reflexive Method in Archaeology.* Ed. I. Hodder. Cambridge: British Institute of Archaeology at Ankara and McDonald Institute.

Ben-zvi, Yael. 2003a. "Setting Instincts: Origin Fictions of Native-Born Settlers." Doctoral dissertation in Modern Thought and Literature, Stanford University.

——. 2003b. "The Spatial and Temporal U.S. of Lewis Henry Morgan's Native America." *Canadian Review of American Studies* 33, no. 3: 211–229.

Bernard, H. Russell 1994. *Research Methods in Anthropology: Qualitative and Quantitative Approaches*, 2nd ed. Thousand Oaks, Calif.: Sage.

Bernstein, Jay. H. 2002. "First Recipients of Anthropological Doctorates in the United States, 1891–1930." *American Anthropologist* 104, no. 2:551–564.

Biagioli, Mario, ed. 1999. *The Science Studies Reader.* New York: Routledge.

Binford, Lewis. 1962. "Archaeology as Anthropology." *American Antiquity* 28:217–225

——. 1971. "Mortuary Practices: Their Study and Their Potential." In *Approaches to the Social Dimensions of Mortuary Practices.* Washington, D.C.: Society for American Archaeology 25.

——. 1989. *Debating Archaeology.* New York: Academic Press.

Bintliff, John, ed. 1991. *The Annales School and Archaeology.* New York: New York University Press.

Bloomfield, Leonard. 1933. *Language.* New York: Holt, Rinehart, and Winston.

Boas, Franz. 1904. "Address at the International Congress of Arts and Science, St. Louis, September." Published in *Congress of Arts and Science* 5:468–482. Ed. H. J. Rogers. Boston: Houghton and Mifflin, 1906. Reprinted in *A Franz Boas Reader: The Shaping of American Anthropology, 1883–1911.* Ed. George W. Stocking Jr. Chicago: University of Chicago Press, 1982.

——. 1912. "Changes in Bodily Form of Descendants of Immigrants." *American Anthropologist*, n.s. 14:530–562.

——. 1940a. [1896]. "The Limitations of the Comparative Method." In *Race, Language, and Culture*, 270–280. New York: Macmillan.

——. 1940b. *Race, Language, and Culture.* New York: Macmillan.

Boon, James A. 1998. "Accenting Hybridity: Postcolonial Cultural Studies, a Boasian Anthropologist, and I." In *"Culture" and the Problem of the Disciplines.* Ed. J. C. Rowe. New York: Columbia University Press.

Boon, James A., and David M. Schneider. 1974. "Kinship vis-à-vis Myth: Contrasts in Levi-Strauss' Approaches to Cross-Cultural Comparison." *American Anthropologist* 76, no. 4:799–817.

Borofsky, Robert. 2002. "The Four Subfields: Anthropologists as Mythmakers." *American Anthropologist* 104, no. 2:463–480.

Bourdieu, Pierre. 1977. *Outline of a Theory of Practice.* Cambridge: Cambridge University Press.

——. 1991. *Language and Symbolic Power.* Ed. John B. Thompson. Trans. Gino Raymond and Matthew Adamson. Cambridge, Mass.: Harvard University Press.

Bourguignon, Erika. 1996. "American Anthropology: A Personal View." *General Anthropology* no. 3, 1:7–9.

Bradley, Richard. 1993. *Altering the Earth: The Origins of Monuments in Britain and Continental Europe.* Edinburgh: Society of Antiquaries of Scotland.

Brenneis, Donald and Ronald Macaulay, eds. 1996. *The Matrix re Language: Contemporary Linguistic Anthropology.* Boulder, Colo: Westview Press.

Brettell, Carol ed. 1993. *When They Read What We Write: The Politics of Ethnography.* London: Bergen and Garvey.

Bright, William, ed. 1966. *Sociolinguistics.* The Hague: Mouton.

Brown, Roger. 1958. *Words and Things.* Glencoe, Ill.: Free Press.

Bruner, Jerome S., Jacqueline J. Goodnow, and George A. Austin. 1956. *A Study of Thinking.* New York: Wiley.

Buchli, Victor. 1999. *An Archaeology of Socialism.* Oxford: Berg.

Buchli, Victor, and Gavin Lucas. 2001. "The Absent Present: Archaeologies of the Contemporary Past." In *Archaeologies of the Contemporary Past.* Ed. V. Buchli and G. Lucas, 3–18. London: Routledge.

Bunzl, Matti. 1996. "Franz Boas and the Humboldtian Tradition: From Volksgeist and Nationalcharakter to an Anthropological Concept of Culture." *In* "Volksgeist as Method and Ethic: Essays on Boasian Ethnography and the German Anthropological Tradition." *History of Anthropology*, vol. 8. Ed. George W. Stocking Jr., 17–78. Madison: University of Wisconsin Press.

Calcagno, James M., ed. 2003 "Special issue: biological anthropology: historical perspectives on current issues, disciplinary connection, and future directions." *American Anthropologist* 105 (1).

Calhoun, Craig. 2002. "Opening remarks: roundtable on rethinking International Studies in a changing global context." *Items and Issues* 3 (3–4): 1, 3–4.

Cantrell, W. Dustin. 2003. "Putting anthropology in schools." *Anthropology News* 44 (4):16.

Caspari, Rachel. 2003. "From Types to Populations: A Century of Race, Physical Anthropology, and the American Anthropological Association." *American Anthropologist* 105 (1): 65–76.

Chagnon, Napoleon A. 1968. *Yanomamö: The Fierce People.* New York: Holt, Reinhart, and Winston.

——. 1983. [1968]. *Yanomamö: The Fierce People*, 3rd ed. New York: Holt, Rinehart, and Winston.

Chakrabarty, Dipesh. 1992. "Postcoloniality and the Artifice of History: Who Speaks for the 'Indian' Pasts?" *Representations* 37, no. 1:1–26.

Chandler, Nahum D. 1996. "The Economy of Desedimentation: W. E. B. DuBois and the Discourses of the Negro." *Callaloo* 19 (1), 78–93.

Chandler, Nahum D. 2000. "Originary Displacement." *Boundary 2* 27 (3): 249–86.

Clarke, David L. 1968. *Analytical Archaeology.* London: Methuen.

Cleere, Henry, ed. 1989. *Archaeological Heritage Management in the Modern World.* London: Unwin Hyman.

Clifford, James. 1997a. *Routes: Travel and Translation in the Late Twentieth Century.* Cambridge, Mass.: Harvard University Press.

——. 1997b. "Spatial Practices: Fieldwork, Travel, and the Disciplining of Anthropology." In *Routes: Travel and Translation in the Late Twentieth Century*, 52–91. Cambridge, Mass.: Harvard University Press.

——. 2000. "Taking Identity Politics Seriously: "The Contradictory, Stony

Ground. . . ." In *Without Guarantees: In Honour of Stuart Hall.* Ed. Paul Gilroy, Lawrence Grossberg, and Angela McRobbie, 94–112. London: Verso.

Clifford, James, and George Marcus, eds. 1986. *Writing Culture: The Poetics of Ethnography.* Berkeley: University of California Press.

Collini, Stefan. 1993. "Introduction," In C. P. Snow, *The Two Cultures* (Canto edition). New York: Cambridge University Press.

Commission to Review the Organizational Structure of the American Anthropological Association. 1997. "Report of the Commission to Review the Organizational Structure of the American Anthropological Association." *Anthropology Newsletter*, December, 8–11.

Cooper, Frederick, and Ann L. Stoler. 1997. *Tensions of Empire: Colonial Cultures in a Bourgeois World.* Berkeley: University of California Press.

Copley, M., K. Clark, and R. Evershed. 2004. "Organic Residues." In *Changing Materialities at Çatalhöyük.* Ed. I. Hodder. Cambridge: British Institute of Archaeology at Ankara and McDonald Institute.

Cosmides, Leda, John Tooby, and Helena Cronin. 2001. *What Is Evolutionary Psychology: Explaining the New Science of the Mind; Darwinism Today.* New Haven: Yale University Press.

Damasio, A. R., et al., eds. 2001. "Unity of Knowledge: The Convergence of Natural and Human Science." *Annals of the New York Academy of Sciences* 935:261–265. New York: New York Academy of Sciences.

Daniel, Glyn. 1962. *The Idea of Prehistory.* Harmondsworth: Penguin.

Darnell, Regna. 2001. *Invisible Genealogies: A History of American Anthropology.* Lincoln: University of Nebraska Press.

De Certeau, M. 1984. *The Practice of Everyday Life.* Berkeley: University of California Press.

Deloria, Philip J. 1998. *Playing Indian.* New Haven: Yale University Press.

Dening, Greg. 1980. *Islands and Beaches: Discourse on a Silent Land: Marquesas 1774–1880.* Honolulu: University of Hawaii Press.

Diamond, Jared. 1997. *Guns, Germs and Steel.* New York: Norton.

DiLeonardo, Micaela. 1991. *Gender at the Crossroads of Knowledge.* Berkeley: University of California.

Dobres, Marcia-Anne. 2000. *Technology and Social Agency.* Oxford: Blackwell.

Dominguez, Virginia. 1996. "Disciplining Anthropology." In *Disciplinarity and Dissent in Cultural Studies.* Ed. Carey Nelson and Dilip Parameshwar Gaonkar, 37–62. New York: Routledge.

Dorian, Nancy C. 1973. "Grammatical Change in a Dying Dialect." *Language* 49:413–438.

———. 1981. *Language Death: The Life Cycle of a Scottish Gaelic Dialect.* Philadelphia: University of Pennsylvania Press.

———, ed. 1989. *Investigating Obsolescence: Studies in Language Contraction and Death.* Cambridge: Cambridge University Press.

Dowson, Thomas, and David Lewis-Williams. 1994. *Contested Images: Diversity in*

Southern African Rock Art Research. Johannesburg: Witwatersrand University Press.

Dresch, Paul, Wendy James, and David Parkin, eds. 2000. *Anthropologists in a Wider World* (*Methodology and History in Anthropology, Vol. 6.* David Parkin, General Editor). New York: Berghahn Books.

Du Bois, W. E. B. 1940. *Dusk of Dawn: An Essay toward an Autobiography of a Race Concept.* New York: Harcourt Brace.

Duchet, Michèle. 1984. *Le Partage des savoirs: Discours historique, discours ethnologique.* Paris: Editions La Découverte.

Dunnell, R. C. 1980. "Evolutionary Theory and Archaeology." In *Advances in Archaeological Method and Theory.* Ed. Michael B. Schiffer, 35–99. New York: Academic Press.

Duranti, Alessandro, ed. 1997. *Linguistic Anthropology: A Reader.* Oxford: Blackwell.

Durham, William. 1998. "Department of Anthropological Sciences: Vision Statement." *Anthropology Newsletter*, October, 21–22.

Earle, Timothy. 1998. "Fashioning a Departmental Identity at Northwestern." Northwestern University, Department of Anthropology, departmental identity statement (www.nwu.edu/anthropology/identity.htm).

Elcock, W. D. 1960. *The Romance Languages.* London: Faber and Faber.

Eldredge, Niles and Stephen J. Gould. 1972. "Punctuated equilibria: an alternative to phyletic gradualism." In *Models in Paleobiology.* Ed. T. Schopf. San Francisco: Freeman, Cooper, and Co.

Elias, Norbert. 1994 [1936]. *The Civilizing Process: The History of Manners.* Oxford: Blackwell.

Ember, Carol, and Melvin Ember. 1990. *Cultural Anthropology*, 6th ed. Englewood Cliffs, N.J.: Prentice Hall.

Erikson, Ken 1999. "Postal Modernism." *Anthropology News*, March, 17–18.

Evans, Christopher, and Caroline Humphrey. 2003. "History, Timelessness and the Monumental: The Oboos of the Mergen Environs, Inner Mongolia." *Cambridge Archaeological Journal* 13: 195–211.

Evans-Pritchard, Edward E. 1965. "The Comparative Method in Social Anthropology." In *The Position of Women in Primitive Societies and Other Essays in Social Anthropology.* London: Faber and Faber.

Fabian, Johannes. 1983. *Time and the Other: How Anthropology Makes Its Object.* New York: Columbia University Press.

Fardon, Richard, ed. 1990. *Localizing Strategies: Regional Traditions of Ethnographic Writing.* Washington: Smithsonian Institution Press.

Feeley-Harnik, Gillian. 2001. "The Ethnography of Creation: Lewis Henry Morgan and the American Beaver." In: *Relative Values: Reconfiguring Kinship.* Ed. Sarah Franklin and Susan McKinnon. Durham: Duke University Press.

Ferguson, Brian. 1995. *Yanomami Warfare.* Santa Fe, N.M.: School of American Research Press.

Fieldhouse, David K. 1982. *The Colonial Empires: A Comparative Survey from the Eighteenth Century*, 2nd ed. London: Macmillan.

Fishman, Joshua A., ed. 1991. *Reversing Language Shift: Theoretical and Empirical Foundations of Assistance to Threatened Languages.* Clevedon: Multilingual Matters.

——. 2001. *Can Threatened Languages Be Saved? Reversing Language Shift, Revisited: A 21st Century Perspective.* Clevedon: Multilingual Matters.

Foley, William. 1997. *Anthropological Linguistics: An Introduction.* Oxford: Blackwell.

Fortes, Meyer. 1970. [1949] "Time and Social Structure: An Ashanti Case Study." In *Time and Social Structure and Other Essays.* London: Athlone Press.

Foucault, Michel 1973. *The Order of Things: An Archaeology of the Human Sciences.* New York: Vintage Books.

Fowler, Peter. 1992. *The Past in Contemporary Society: Then, Now.* London: Routledge.

Fox, Richard, ed. 1991. *Recapturing Anthropology: Working in the Present.* Santa Fe, N.M.: School of American Research Press.

Fox, Richard, and Barbara King. 2002. "Introduction: Beyond Culture Worry." In *Anthropology beyond Culture.* Ed. Richard Fox and Barbara King, 1–22. Oxford: Berg.

Fredrickson, George. 1988. *The Arrogance of Race: Historical Perspectives on Slavery, Racism, and Social Inequality.* Middletown, Conn.: Wesleyan University Press.

Gal, Susan, and Kathryn A. Woolard, eds. 2001. *Languages and Publics: The Making of Authority.* Manchester: St. Jerome Publishing.

Galison, Peter. 1997. *Image and Logic: A Material Culture of Microphysics.* Chicago: University of Chicago Press.

Gallie, W. B. 1964. *Philosophy and the Historical Understanding.* London: Chatto and Windus.

Geertz, Clifford. 1962 [1973]. "The Growth of Culture and the Evolution of Mind." In *The Interpretation of Cultures.* New York: Basic Books.

——. 1964. "The Transition to Humanity." In *Horizons of Anthropology.* Ed. S. Tax, 37–48. Chicago: Aldine.

——. 1973. *The Interpretation of Cultures.* New York: Basic Books.

——. 1983. *Local Knowledge: Further Essays in Interpretive Anthropology.* New York: Basic Books.

——. 1984. "Anti Anti-relativism." *American Anthropologist* 86:263–278.

Gero, Joan, and Margaret Conkey. 1991. *Engendering Archaeology.* Oxford: Blackwell.

Geuss, Raymond. 1981. *The Idea of a Critical Theory: Habermas and the Frankfurt School.* Cambridge: Cambridge University Press.

Gieryn, Thomas F. 1999. *Cultural Boundaries of Science: Credibility on the Line.* Chicago: University of Chicago Press.

Gillespie, Susan D., Deborah L. Nichols, and Rosemary A. Joyce. 2003. "The Future of Archaeological Anthropology." *Anthropology News* 44 (4):4–5.

Gilroy, Paul. 1990. "One Nation under a Groove: The Cultural Politics of 'Race' and Racism in Britain." In *Anatomy of Racism.* Ed. David Theo Goldberg. Minneapolis: University of Minnesota Press.

——. 1991 [1987]. *There Ain't No Black in the Union Jack: The Cultural Politics of Race and Nation.* Chicago: University of Chicago Press.

——. 2000. *Against Race: Imagining Political Culture beyond the Color Line.* Cambridge, Mass.: Harvard University Press.

Glanz, J. 2001. "To Be Young and in Search of the Higgs Boson." *New York Times*, July 24, F3.

Ginsburg, Faye, and Rayna Rapp, eds. 1995. *Conceiving the New World Order.* Berkeley: University of California Press.

Goldberg, David Theo. 1993. *Racist Culture: Philosophy and the Politics of Meaning.* Oxford: Blackwell.

——. 1997. *Racial Subjects.* New York: Routledge.

——. 2002. *The Racial State.* Oxford: Blackwell.

Goldberg, David Theo, ed. 1990. *Anatomy of Racism.* Minneapolis: University of Minnesota Press.

Goldschmidt, Walter. 2000. "Historical Essay: A Perspective on Anthropology." *American Anthropologist* 102, no. 4:789–807.

Goodenough, Ward H. 1970. *Description and Comparison in Cultural Anthropology.* Chicago: Aldine.

Goodman, Alan. 2001. "Biological Diversity and Cultural Diversity: From Race to Radical Bioculturalism." In *Cultural Diversity in the United States.* Ed. I. Susser and T. Patterson. Oxford: Blackwell.

Gosden, Chris. 1999. *Anthropology and Archaeology: A Changing Relationship.* London: Routledge.

Graff, Gerald. 1987. *Professing Literature: An Institutional History.* Chicago: University of Chicago Press.

Greenberg, Joseph H. 1966. "Language Universals." In *Current Trends in Linguistics*, vol. 3: *Theoretical Foundations.* Ed. Thomas A. Sebeok, 61–112. The Hague: Mouton.

Greenblatt, Stephen. 1999. "The Touch of the Real." In *The Fate of "Culture": Geertz and Beyond.* Ed. S. Ortner. 30–34. Berkeley: University of California Press.

Gregory, Derek. 1994. *Geographical Imaginations.* Oxford: Blackwell.

Gross, Paul, and Norman Levitt. 1994. *Higher Superstition.* Baltimore: Johns Hopkins University Press.

Gumperz, John J. 1968. "Linguistics: The Speech Community." In *International Encyclopedia of the Social Sciences*, vol. 9. Ed. David L. Sills, 381–386. New York: Macmillan and Free Press.

Gumperz, John J., and Dell H. Hymes, eds. 1964. "The Ethnography of Communication." *American Anthropologist* 66, no. 6, part 2.

——. eds. 1972. *Directions in Sociolinguistics: The Ethnography of Communication.* New York: Holt, Reinhart, and Winston.

Gupta, Akhil, and James Ferguson, eds. 1997. *Anthropological Locations: Boundaries and Grounds of a Field Science.* Berkeley: University of California Press.

Hafner, K. 1999. "Coming of Age in Palo Alto." *New York Times,* June 10, G1, 8.

Hall, Stuart. 1996. "On Postmodernism and Articulation: An Interview with Stuart Hall." Reprinted in *Stuart Hall: Critical Dialogues in Cultural Studies,* ed. Dana Marley and Kuan-Hsing Chen, 131–150. London: Routledge.

Hamann, Byron. 2002. "The Social Life of Pre-Sunrise Things: Indigenous Mesoamerican Archaeology." *Current Anthropology* 43:351–382.

Hannerz, Ulf. 1996. *Transnational Connections: Culture, People, Places.* New York: Routledge.

Haraway, Donna. 1991. *Simians, Cyborgs and Women.* New York: Routledge.

Harris, Marvin. 1968. *The Rise of Anthropological Theory: A History of Theories of Culture.* New York: Crowell.

———. 1979. *Cultural Materialism: The Struggle for a Science of Culture.* New York: Random House.

———. 1999. *Theories of Culture in Postmodern Times.* Walnut Creek, Calif.: Alta Mira Press.

Harrison, Faye. 1998a. "Introduction: Expanding the Discourse on "Race."" *American Anthropologist* 100, no. 3:609–631.

———. ed. 1998b. "Race and Racism." Special "Contemporary Issues Forum" issue. *American Anthropologist* 100, no.3.

Herrnstein, Richard J., and Charles Murray. 1994. *The Bell Curve: Intelligence and Class Structure in American Life.* New York: Free Press.

Herzfeld, Michael. 1987. *Anthropology through the Looking-Glass: Critical Ethnography in the Margins of Europe.* Cambridge: Cambridge University Press.

Hicks, David, and Margaret Gwynne. 1996. *Cultural Anthropology,* 2nd ed. New York: Harper Collins.

Hill, Jane H., Nancy C. Dorian, Nora C. England, Joshua A. Fishman, and Leanne Hinton. 2002. "'Expert Rhetorics' in Advocacy for Endangered Languages: Who Is Listening, and What Do They Hear?" [With commentaries.] *Journal of Linguistic Anthropology* 12:119–156.

Hinsley, Curtis M., Jr. 1992. "The Museum Origins of Harvard Anthropology 1866–1915." In *Science at Harvard University: Historical Perspectives.* Ed. Clark A. Elliott and Margaret W. Rossiter, 12–45. Bethlehem, Pa.: Lehigh University Press.

Hinton, Leanne, and Ken Hale, eds. 2001. *The Green Book of Language Revitalization in Practice.* San Diego, Calif.: Academic Press.

Hobsbawm, Eric, and Terence Ranger, eds. 1983. *The Invention of Tradition.* Cambridge: Cambridge University Press.

Hodder, Ian. 1986. *Reading the Past.* Cambridge: Cambridge University Press.

———. 1999. *The Archaeological Process.* Oxford: Blackwell.

———. ed. 2001. *Archaeological Theory Today.* Cambridge: Polity.

Holloway, Ralph. 1969. "Culture: A Human Domain." *Current Anthropology* 10, no. 4:395–412.

Holm, John A. 1988–1989. *Pidgins and Creoles*, 2 vols. Cambridge: Cambridge University Press.

Holton, Gerald. 1993. *Science and Antiscience.* Cambridge, MA: Harvard University Press.

Holy, Ladislau. 1987a. "Introduction: Description, Generalization and Comparison: Two Paradigms." In *Comparative Anthropology.* Ed. L. Holy. New York: Blackwell.

——, ed. 1987b. *Comparative Anthropology.* New York: Blackwell.

Huddleston, Rodney D. 1974. "Componential Analysis: The Sememe and the Concept of Distinctiveness." *Canadian Journal of Linguistics* 19:1–17.

Huffman, T. N. 1984. "Expressive Space in the Zimbabwe Culture." *Man* 19:593–612.

Hymes, Dell H., ed. 1971. *Pidginization and Creolization of Languages: Proceedings of a Conference Held at the University of the West Indies, Mona, Jamaica, April 1968.* Cambridge: Cambridge University Press.

Ingold, Tim. 1996a. "General Introduction." In *Key Debates in Anthropology.* Ed. T. Ingold. New York: Routledge.

——, ed. 1996b. *Key Debates in Anthropology.* New York: Routledge.

Jakobson, Roman. 1978. *Six Lectures on Sound and Meaning.* Trans. John Mepham. Cambridge, Mass.: MIT Press.

James, Wendy. 2002 "The Anthropological Family: From Ancestors to Affines." Presidential Address. Royal Anthropological Institute, 26 June 2002.

Jensen, Arthur. 1969. "How Much Can We Boost IQ and Scholastic Achievement?" *Harvard Educational Review* 39 (1):1–123.

Johnson, Matthew. 1996. *An Archaeology of Capitalism.* London: Blackwell.

——. 1999. *Archaeological Theory: An Introduction.* London: Blackwell.

Jolly, Margaret. 1993. "Colonizing Women: The Maternal Body and Empire." In *Feminism and the Politics of Difference.* Ed. Sneda Gunew and Ana Yeatman. Boulder, Colo.: Westview Press.

Jones, Martin. 2001. *The Molecule Hunt: Archaeology and the Search for Ancient DNA.* London: Allen Lane.

Joyce, Rosemary. 2002. *The Languages of Archaeology.* London: Blackwell.

Kirch, Patrick, and Marshall Sahlins. 1992. *Anahulu: The Anthropology of History in the Kingdom of Hawaii.* Chicago: University of Chicago Press.

Klein, Julie Thompson. 1996. *Crossing Boundaries: Knowledge, Disciplinarities, Interdisciplinarities.* Charlottesville: University of Virginia Press.

Knapp, A. Bernard, ed. 1992. *Archaeology, Annales and Ethnohistory.* Cambridge: Cambridge University Press.

Köbben, Andre J. 1970. "Comparatives and Non-Comparatives in Anthropology." In *Handbook of Method in Cultural Anthropology.* Ed. R. Naroll and R. Cohen. New York: Natural History Press.

Kottak, Conrad Phillip. 1975. *Cultural Anthropology.* New York: Random House.

——. 2004. *Cultural Anthropology*, 10th ed. New York: McGraw Hill.

Kroeber, Alfred L. 1952. *The Nature of Culture.* Chicago: University of Chicago Press.

Kroeber, Alfred L., and Clyde Kluckhohn. 1952. *Culture: A Critical Review of Concepts and Definitions.* New York: Vintage.

Kroskrity, Paul V., ed. 2000. *Regimes of Language: Ideologies, Polities, and Identities.* Santa Fe, N.M.: School of American Research Press.

Kuhn, Thomas. 1996 [1962]. *The Structure of Scientific Revolutions*, 3rd ed. Chicago: University of Chicago Press.

Kuper, Adam. 1988. *The Invention of Primitive Society.* London: Routledge.

Labov, William. 1972. *Sociolinguistic Patterns.* Philadelphia: University of Pennsylvania Press.

——. 2001. *Principles of Linguistic Change*, vol. 2: *Social Factors.* Oxford: Blackwell.

Latour, Bruno, 1993. *We Have Never Been Modern.* Cambridge: Harvard University Press.

Lechtman, H. 1996. "The Andean World; Cloth and Metal: The Culture of Technology." In *Andean Art at Dumbarton Oaks.* Ed. E. Boone, 15–43. Washington: Dumbarton Oaks.

Lederman, R. 1998. "Globalization and the Future of 'Culture Areas': Melanesian Anthropology in Transition." *Annual Review of Anthropology* 28.

——. n.d. "From Somewhere: Relocating Anthropology's Regional Traditions." In *A New History of Anthropology.* Ed. Henrika Kuklick. New York: Blackwell.

Lee, Richard, and Irven DeVore, eds. 1968. *Man the Hunter.* Chicago: Aldine.

Lemonnier, Pierre. 1986. "The Study of Material Culture Today: Towards an Anthropology of Technical Systems." *Journal of Anthropological Archaeology* 5:147–186.

Lévi-Strauss, Claude. 1949. *Les Structures élémentaires de la parenté.* Paris: Presses universitaires de France.

——. 1958. *Anthropologie structurale.* Paris: Plon.

——. 1966. *The Savage Mind.* [Translator not identified.] Chicago: University of Chicago Press.

——. 1973. *Anthropologie structurale deux.* Paris: Plon.

Lewis, M. 2001. "Faking It." *New York Times*, magazine section, July 15, 32–62.

Lindstrom, Lamont, and Peter Stromberg. 1999. "Beyond the 'Savage Slot.'" *Anthropology News*, November, 9–10.

Liss, Julia. 1998. "Diasporic Identities: The Science and Politics of Race in the Work of Franz Boas and W. E. B. DuBois, 1894–1919." *Cultural Anthropology* 13, no. 2:127–166.

Liu, Alan. 1998. "The Downsizing of Knowledge: Knowledge Work and Literary History." In *Knowledge Work, Literary History, and the Future of Literary Studies*, 1–22. Berkeley: University of California. Occasional Papers of the Townsend Center for the Humanities, No. 15.

——. 2004. *The Laws of Cool: Knowledge Work and the Culture of Information.* Chicago: University of Chicago Press.

Longacre, William. 1970. *Archaeology as Anthropology.* Tucson: Anthropological Papers of the University of Arizona 17.

Lorenz, Konrad. 1966. *On Aggression.* New York: Harcourt, Brace and World.

Lounsbury, Floyd G. 1956. "A Semantic Analysis of the Pawnee Kinship Usage." *Language* 32:158–194.

———. 1969a. [1964]. "A Formal Account of the Crow- and Omaha-Type Kinship Terminologies." In *Cognitive Anthropology.* Ed. Stephen A. Tyler, 212–255. New York: Holt, Rinehart, and Winston.

———. 1969b. [1964]. "The Structural Analysis of Kinship Semantics." In *Cognitive Anthropology.* Ed. Stephen A. Tyler, 193–212. New York: Holt, Rinehart, and Winston.

Lowenthal, David. 1985. *The Past Is a Foreign Country.* Cambridge: Cambridge University Press.

Lowie, Robert. 1937. *The History of Ethnological Theory.* New York: Farrar and Rinehart.

Lucy, John A. 1992. *Language Diversity and Thought: A Reformulation of the Linguistic Relativity Hypothesis.* Cambridge: Cambridge University Press.

———. 1996. "The Scope of Linguistic Relativity: An Analysis and Review of Empirical Research." In *Rethinking Linguistic Relativity.* Ed. John J. Gumperz and Stephen C. Levinson, 37–69. Cambridge: Cambridge University Press.

———. 1997. "The Linguistics of 'Color.'" In *Color Categories in Thought and Languages.* Ed. C. L. Hardin and Luisa Maffi, 320–346. Cambridge: Cambridge University Press.

Lumsden, Charles J., and Edward O. Wilson. 1981. *Genes, Mind, and Culture: The Coevolutionary Process.* Cambridge, Mass.: Harvard University Press.

Lynch, M. 2000. "Against Reflexivity as an Academic Virtue and Source of Privileged Knowledge." *Theory, Culture and Society* 17, no. 3:26–54.

MacClancy, Jeremy, ed. 2002. *Exotic No More: Anthropology on the Front Lines.* Chicago: University of Chicago Press.

Malinowski, Bronislaw. 1922. *Argonauts of the Western Pacific: An Account of Native Enterprise and Adventure in the Archipelagoes of Melanesian New Guinea.* London: G. Routledge and Sons.

Marcus, George. 1992. "Cultural Anthropology at Rice since the 1980s." Provost lecture, February 17, 1992 (www.ruf.rice.edu/~anth/provost.html).

———. 1995. "Ethnography in/of the World System: The Emergence of Multi-Sited Ethnography." *Annual Review of Anthropology* 24:95–117. Palo Alto: Annual Reviews.

———. 1999a. "Postmodernist critique in the 1980s, nuclear diplomacy, and the 'prisoner's dilemma.'" In *Critical Anthropology Now.* Ed. George Marcus. Santa Fe: SAR Press.

———. 1999b. "The uses of complicity in the changing mise-en-scène of anthropological fieldwork." In *The Fate of "Culture": Geertz and Beyond.* Ed. Sherry B. Ortner. Berkeley: University of California Press.

Marcus, George, and Michael Fischer. 1986. *Anthropology as Cultural Critique.* Chicago: University of Chicago Press.

Martin, Emily. 1994. *Flexible Bodies: Tracking Immunity in America from the Days of Polio to the Age of AIDS.* Boston: Beacon.

——. 1995. "From Reproduction to HIV: Blurring Categories, Shifting Positions." In *Conceiving the New World Order*. Ed. Faye Ginsburg and Rayna Rapp. Berkeley: University of California Press.

——. 2000. "Mind-Body Problems." *American Ethnologist* 27, no. 3:569–590.

Mead, Margaret, ed. 1959. *An Anthropologist at Work: Writings of Ruth Benedict*. Boston: Houghton Mifflin.

Meillet, Antoine. 1922. *Linguistique historique et linguistique générale*. Paris: Librairie Honoré Champion.

——. 1936. *Linguistique historique et linguistique générale*, vol. 2. Paris: Librarie C. Klincksieck.

Menand, Louis. 2001. *The Metaphysical Club*. New York: Farrar Straus and Giroux.

Merriman, Nick. 1991. *Beyond the Glass Case*. Leicester: Leicester University Press.

Meskell, Lynn. 2002. "The Intersections of Identity and Politics in Archaeology." *Annual Review of Anthropology* 31:279–301.

Miller, Daniel. 1987. *Material Culture and Mass Consumption*. Oxford: Blackwell.

Miller, Daniel, and Chris Tilley. 1984. *Ideology, Power and Prehistory*. Cambridge: Cambridge University Press.

Miller, George A. 1951. *Language and Communication*. New York: McGraw-Hill.

Moore, Donald S., Jake Kosek, and Anand Pandian, eds. 2003. *Race, Nature and the Politics of Difference*. Durham, N.C.: Duke University Press.

Moore, Frank W. 1961. *Readings in Cross-Cultural Methodology*. New Haven: Human Relations Area Files Press.

Morgan, Lewis Henry. 1870. *Systems of Consanguinity and Affinity of the Human Family*. Washington, D.C. Smithsonian Institution.

——. 1954. *League of the Ho-de'-no-sau-nee, or Iroquois*. New Haven: Human Relations Area Files.

——. 1985 [1877]. *Ancient Society: Or, Researches in the Lines of Human Progress from Savagery through Barbarism to Civilization*. Tucson: University of Arizona Press.

Morpurgo-Davies, Anna. 1994. *History of Linguistics*. Ed. Giulio Lepschy. Vol. 4: *Nineteenth-Century Linguistics*. London: Longman.

Morris, Ian. 2000. *Archaeology as Cultural History*. Oxford: Blackwell.

Moses, Yolanda T. 1997. "Are Four Fields in Our Future?" *Anthropology Newsletter*, December, 8.

Mühlhäusler, Peter. 1986. *Pidgin and Creole Linguistics*. Oxford: Blackwell.

Mukhopadhyay, C. C., and Y. T. Moses. 1997. "Reestablishing 'Race' in Anthropological Discourse." *American Anthropologist* 99, no. 3:517–533.

Murdock, George Peter. 1949. *Social Structure*. New York: Macmillan.

——. 1971. *Outline of Cultural Materials*, 4th ed. New Haven: Human Relations Area Files Press.

Nader, Laura. 1969. "Up the Anthropologist: Perspectives Gained from Studying Up." In *Reinventing Anthropology*. Ed. Dell Hymes, 284–311. New York: Vintage.

Nanda, Serena. 1987. *Cultural Anthropology*, 3rd ed. Belmont, Calif.: Wadsworth.

Nanda, Serena, and Richard Warms. 2002. *Cultural Anthropology*, 7th ed. Belmont, Calif.: Wadsworth.

Novick, Peter. 1988. *That Noble Dream: The "Objectivity Question" and the American Historical Profession.* Cambridge: Cambridge University Press.

Nugent, Stephen. 2001. "Anthropology and Public Culture: The Yanomami, Science and Ethics." *Anthropology Today* no. 17, 3:10–14.

Olsen, B. 2003. "Material Culture after Text: Re-membering Things." *Norwegian Archaeological Review* 36: 88–104.

Ong, Walter J. 1982. *Orality and Literary: The Technologizing of the Word.* London: Methuen.

Orme, Bryony. 1981. *Anthropology for Archaeologists: An Introduction.* London: Duckworth.

Ortner, Sherry. 1984. "Theory in Anthropology since the Sixties." *Comparative Studies in Society and History* 26: 126–166.

——, ed. 1999a. *The Fate of "Culture": Geertz and Beyond.* Berkeley: University of California Press. Representations Books 8.

——. 1999b. "Introduction." In *The Fate of "Culture": Geertz and Beyond.* Ed. S. Ortner. Berkeley: University of California Press. Representations Books 8.

Otterbein, Keith. 1999. "A History of Research on Warfare in Anthropology." *American Anthropologist* 101, no. 4:794–805.

Parker Pearson, Michael. 1982. "Mortuary Practices, Society and Ideology: An Ethnoarchaeological Study." In *Symbolic and Structural Archaeology.* Ed. I. Hodder. Cambridge: Cambridge University Press.

——. 2002 *In Search of the Red Slave.* Sutton: Stroud.

Patterson, Thomas. 2001. *A Social History of Anthropology in the U.S.* Oxford: Berg.

Paul, Robert, ed. 1987. "Biological and Cultural Anthropology at Emory University." Special issue. *Cultural Anthropology* 2, no. 1.

Pearson, M., and Sullivan S. 1999. *Looking after Heritage Places.* Melbourne: Melbourne University Press.

Peel, J. D. Y. 1987. "History, Culture and the Comparative Method: A West African Puzzle." In *Comparative Anthropology.* Ed. L. Holy. New York: Blackwell.

Peregrine, Peter N., Carol R. Ember and Melvin Ember, eds. 2002. *Physical Anthropology: Original Readings in Method and Practice.* Upper Saddle River, NJ: Prentice Hall.

Phillips, Mark. Forthcoming. "What Is Tradition When It Is Not Invented?" In *The Question of Tradition: Exploring the Idea of Tradition across the Disciplines.* Ed. Mark Phillips and Gordon Schochet. Toronto: University of Toronto Press.

Pike, Kenneth. 1967. *Language in Relation to a Unified Theory of the Structure of Human Behavior*, 2nd ed., rev. The Hague: Mouton. [Original, 3 vols., 1954–1960.]

Pinker, Steven. 2002. *The Blank Slate: The Modern Denial of Human Nature.* New York: Viking.

Plog, Fred, and Daniel Bates. 1976. *Cultural Anthropology.* New York: Knopf.

——. 1980. *Cultural Anthropology*, 2nd ed. New York: Knopf.

Rabinow, Paul. 1977. *Reflections on Fieldwork in Morocco*. Berkeley: University of California Press.

——. 1996. *Making PCR: A Story of Biotechnology*. Chicago: University of Chicago Press.

——. 1999. "American Moderns: On Sciences and Scientists." In *Critical Anthropology Now*. Ed. G. Marcus. Santa Fe: SAR Press.

Rathje, Bill. 1979. "Modern Material Culture Studies." *Advances in Archaeological Method and Theory* 2:1–27.

Reiter, Rayna R., ed. 1975. *Toward an Anthropology of Women*. New York: Monthly Review Press.

Renfrew, Colin. 1987. *Archaeology and Language*. London: Jonathan Cape.

——, ed. 2000. *Archaeogenetics. DNA and the Population History of Europe*. Cambridge: McDonald Institute for Archaeological Research.

Romaine, Susanne. 1988. *Pidgin and Creole Languages*. London: Longman.

Rosaldo, Michelle, and Louise Lamphere, eds. 1974. *Women, Culture and Society*. Stanford: Stanford University Press.

Rosaldo, Renato. 1980. *Ilongot Headhunting 1883–1974*. Stanford: Stanford University Press.

——. 1999. "A Note on Geertz as a Cultural Essayist." In *The Fate of "Culture": Geertz and Beyond*. Ed. S. Ortner. Berkeley: University of California Press. Representations Books 8.

Ross, Andrew, ed. 1996. *Science Wars*. Durham: Duke University Press.

Sahlins, Marshall. 1972. *Stone Age Economics*. New York: Aldine.

——. 1976. *The Use and Abuse of Biology: An Anthropological Critique of Sociobiology*. Ann Arbor: University of Michigan Press.

——. 1981. *Historical Metaphors and Mythical Realities*. Ann Arbor: University of Michigan Press.

——. 1985. *Islands of History*. Chicago: University of Chicago Press.

——. 2000a. *Culture in Practice: Selected Essays*. New York: Zone Books.

——. 2000b. "What Is Anthropological Enlightenment? Some Lessons of the Twentieth Century." In *Culture in Practice: Selected Essays*, 501–526. New York: Zone Books.

——. 2000c. "Goodbye to *Tristes Tropes*: Ethnography in the Context of Modern World History." In *Culture in Practice: Selected Essays* (2000), 471–500.

Schieffelin, Bambi, Kathryn A. Woolard, and Paul V. Kroskrity, eds. 1998. *Language Ideologies: Practice and Theory*. New York: Oxford University Press.

Schiffer, Michael B. 1976. *Behavioral Archaeology*. New York: Academic Press.

——. 1999. *The Material Life of Human Beings*. London: Routledge.

——, ed. 2000. *Social Theory in Archaeology*. Salt Lake City: University of Utah Press.

Schmidt, P. 1997. *Iron Technology in East Africa: Symbolism, Science, and Archaeology*. Bloomington: University of Indiana Press.

Schneider, David Murray. 1968. *American Kinship: A Cultural Account*. Englewood Cliffs, N.J.: Prentice-Hall.

——. 1984. *A Critique of the Study of Kinship.* Ann Arbor: University of Michigan Press.

Segal, Daniel. 1999. "Ethnographic Classics, Ethnographic Examples: Some Thoughts on the New Cultural Studies and an Old Queer Science." In *Kulturstudien heute (The contemporary study of culture).* Ed. I. Korneck et al. Vienna: Turia and Kant.

——. 2000. "'Western Civ' and the Staging of History in American Higher Education." *American Historical Review* 105, no. 3:770–805.

——. n.d. "Western Civ and Its Aftermaths: The Staging of History in American Higher Education."

Seife, R. 2001. "Plans for Next Big Collider Reach Critical Mass at Snowmass." *Science* 293:582.

Seizer, Susan. 1995. "Paradoxes of Visibility in the Field: Rites of Queer Passage in Anthropology." *Public Culture* 8, no. 1:73–100.

Sewell, William H. 1999. "Geertz, Cultural Systems, and History: From Synchrony to Transformation." In *The Fate of "Culture": Geertz and Beyond.* Ed. S. Ortner, 30–34. Berkeley: University of California Press. Representations Books 8.

Shankland, David. 1996. "The Anthropology of an Archaeological Presence." In *On the Surface.* Ed. I. Hodder. Cambridge: British Institute of Archaeology at Ankara and McDonald Institute.

Shanklin, Eugenia. 1998. "The Profession of the Color Blind: Sociocultural Anthropology and Racism in the 21st Century." *American Anthropologist* 100(3) 669–679.

Shanks, M., and Tilley, C. 1987. *Reconstructing Archaeology.* Cambridge: Cambridge University Press.

Shapin, Steven. 1994. *A Social History of Truth: Civility and Science in Seventeenth-Century England.* Chicago: University of Chicago Press.

Silverstein, Michael. 1972. "Chinook Jargon: Language Contact and the Problem of Multi-Level Generative Systems." *Language* 48:378–406 (part 1); 596–625 (part 2).

——. 1996. "Encountering Language and Languages of Encounter in North American Ethnohistory." *Journal of Linguistic Anthropology* 6:126–144.

——. 1997. "Dynamics of Linguistic Contact." In *Handbook of North American Indians,* vol. 17: *Languages.* Ed. I. Goddard, 117–136. Washington, D.C.: Smithsonian Institution Press.

——. 1998. "Contemporary Transformations of Local Linguistic Communities." *Annual Review of Anthropology* 27:401–426.

Silverstein, Michael, and Greg Urban, eds. 1996. *Natural Histories of Discourse.* Chicago: University of Chicago Press.

Snow, C. P. 1993 [1959]. *The Two Cultures* (Canto edition). Cambridge: Cambridge University Press.

Spears, Arthur K., and Donald Winford, eds. 1997. *The Structure and Status of Pidgins and Creoles.* Amsterdam: John Benjamins.

Spiro, Melford E. 1982. *Oedipus in the Trobriands.* Chicago: University of Chicago Press.

Stasiulis, Daiva, and Nira Yuval-Davis. 1995. "Introduction: Beyond Dichotomies: Gender, Race, Ethnicity and Class in Settler Societies." In *Unsettling Settler Societies: Articulations of Gender, Race, Ethnicity and Class.* Ed. D. Stasiulis and N. Yuval-Davis. London: Sage.

Steward, Julian Haynes. 1955. *Theory of Culture Change: The Methodology of Multilinear Evolution.* Urbana: University of Illinois Press.

Stillman, Robert E. 1995. *The New Philosophy and Universal Languages in Seventeenth-Century England: Bacon, Hobbes, and Wilkins.* Lewisburg, Pa.: Bucknell University Press.

Stocking, George W., Jr. 1960. "Franz Boas and the Founding of the American Anthropological Association." *American Anthropologist* 62:1–17.

———. 1968. *Race, Culture and Evolution.* Chicago: University of Chicago Press.

———. 1974. "Introduction: The Basic Assumptions of Boasian Anthropology." In *A Franz Boas Reader: The Shaping of American Anthropology, 1883–1911.* Chicago: University of Chicago Press.

———. 1979. *Anthropology at Chicago: Tradition, Discipline, Department.* An exhibition marking the fiftieth anniversary of the Department of Anthropology. October 1979–February 1980. Chicago: University of Chicago, Joseph Regenstein Library.

———. 1987. *Victorian Anthropology.* New York: Basic Books.

———. 1988. "Guardians of the Sacred Bundle: The American Anthropological Association and the Representation of Holistic Anthropology." In *Learned Societies and the Evolution of the Disciplines.* New York: American Council of Learned Societies.

———. 1992a. "Ideas and Institutions in American Anthropology: Thoughts toward a History of the Interwar Years." In *The Ethnographer's Magic and Other Essays in the History of Anthropology,* 114–177. Madison: University of Wisconsin Press.

———. 1992b. "Paradigmatic Traditions in the History of Anthropology." In *The Ethnographer's Magic and Other Essays in the History of Anthropology,* 342–361. Madison: University of Wisconsin Press.

———. 1995. *After Tylor: British Social Anthropology, 1888–1951.* Madison: University of Wisconsin Press.

———. 1996. "Boasian Ethnography and the German Anthropological Tradition." In "Volksgeist as Method and Ethic: Essays on Boasian Ethnography and the German Anthropological Tradition." *History of Anthropology,* vol. 8. Ed. George W. Stocking Jr., 3–8. Madison: University of Wisconsin Press.

Strathern, Marilyn. 1981. "No Nature, No Culture: The Hagen Case." In *Nature, Culture and Gender.* Ed. C. McCormack and M. Strathern. New York: Cambridge University Press.

———. 1987. "An Awkward Relationship: The Case of Feminism and Anthropology." *Signs* 112, no. 2:276–292.

———. 1989. *The Gender of the Gift.* Berkeley: University of California Press.

Susser, Ida, and Thomas Patterson, eds. 2000. *Cultural Diversity in the United States.* Oxford: Blackwell.

Swadesh, Morris. 1948. "Sociologic Notes on Obsolescent Languages." *International Journal of American Linguistics* 14:226–235.

Tattersall, Ian. 1995. *The Fossil Trail: How We Know What We Think We Know about Human Evolution.* New York: Oxford University Press.

Thomas, Julian. 1996. *Time, Culture and Identity.* London: Routledge.

——, ed. 2001. *Interpretive Archaeology: A Reader.* Leicester: Leicester University Press.

Thomas, Nicholas. 1991. *Entangled Objects: Exchange, Material Culture, and Colonialism in the Pacific.* Cambridge, Mass: Harvard University Press.

Thomason, Sarah G., ed. 1997. *Contact Languages: A Wider Perspective.* Amsterdam: John Benjamins

Thorne, Alan and Milford Wolpoff. 1981. "Regional Continuity in Australasian Pleistocene Hominid Evolution." *American Journal of Physical Anthropology* 65: 337–349.

Thornton, Robert. 1988. "The Rhetoric of Ethnographic Holism." *Cultural Anthropology* 3, no. 3:285–303.

Tierney, Patrick. 2000. *Darkness in El Dorado: How Scientists and Journalists Devastated the Amazon.* New York: Norton.

Tiger, Lionel. 1969. *Men in Groups.* New York: Random House.

Tilley, Christopher, ed. 1993. *Interpretative Archaeology.* Oxford: Berg.

——. 1996. *An Ethnography of the Neolithic.* Cambridge: Cambridge University Press.

——. 1999. *Metaphor and Material Culture.* Oxford: Blackwell.

Tomlinson, John. 1999. *Globalization and Culture.* Oxford: Polity.

Trautmann, Thomas. 1987. *Lewis Henry Morgan and the Invention of Kinship.* Berkeley: University of California Press.

——. 1997. *Aryans and British India.* Berkeley: University of California Press.

Trigger, Bruce 1984. "Alternative Archaeologies: Nationalist, Colonialist, Imperialist." *Man* 19:355–370.

——. 1989. *History of Archaeological Thought.* Cambridge: Cambridge University Press.

Tringham, Ruth. 1994. "Engendered Places in Prehistory." *Gender, Place, and Culture* 1, no. 2:169–204.

Trouillot, Michel-Rolfe. 1991. "Anthropology and the Savage Slot: The Poetics and Politics of Otherness." In *Recapturing Anthropology: Working in the Present.* Ed. Richard Fox, 17–44. Santa Fe, N.M.: School of American Research Press.

Tsing, Anna. 1993. *In the Realm of the Diamond Queen: Marginality in an Out-of-the-Way Place.* Princeton: Princeton University Press.

Tylor, Edward B. 1888. "On a Method of Investigating the Development of Institutions, Applied to Laws of Marriage and Descent." *Journal of the Anthropological Institute of Great Britain and Ireland* 18:245–272.

Ucko, Peter, ed. 1995. *Theory in Archaeology: A World Perspective.* London: Routledge.

Valdman, Albert, ed. 1977. *Pidgin and Creole Linguistics.* Bloomington: Indiana University Press.

Vitalis, Robert. 2002. "International Studies in America." *Items and Issues* 3 (3–4): 1–2, 12–16.

Voss, Barbara, and Robert Schmidt, eds. 2000. *Archaeologies of Sexuality.* New York: Routledge.

Wagner, Roy. 1981. *The Invention of Culture.* Chicago: University of Chicago Press.

Wallman, Joel. 1992. *Aping Language.* New York: Cambridge University Press.

Watkins, J. 2000. *Indigenous Archaeology: American Indian Values and Scientific Practice.* Alta Walnut Creek, Calif.: Mira Press.

Weber, Max. 1958. "Science as a Vocation." In *From Max Weber.* Ed. and trans. Hans Gerth and C. Wright Mills. New York: Oxford University Press.

Weinberg, Steven 1993. *Dreams of a Final Theory.* New York: Vintage.

Weinreich, Uriel. 1954. "Is a Structural Dialectology Possible?" *Word* 10:388–400.

Weinreich, Uriel, William Labov, and Marvin I. Herzog. 1968. "Empirical Foundations for a Theory of Language Change." In *Directions for Historical Linguistics: A Symposium.* Ed. Winfred P. Lehmann and Yakov Malkiel, 95–195. Austin: University of Texas Press.

White, Hayden. 1978. *Tropics of Discourse: Essays in Cultural Criticism.* Baltimore: Johns Hopkins University Press.

White, Leslie A. 1955 *Ethnological Essays.* Ed. Beth Dillingham and Robert L. Carneiro. Albuquerque: University of New Mexico Press.

——. 1959. *The Evolution of Culture: The Development of Civilization to the Fall of Rome.* New York: McGraw-Hill.

Whitehead, Neil 2000. "A History of Research on Warfare in Anthropology: Reply to Keith Otterbein." *American Anthropologist* 102, no. 4:834–837.

Whitley, D. S. 1998. *Reader in Archaeological Theory: Post-processual and Cognitive Approaches.* London: Routledge.

Whitney, W. D. 1971 [1882]. *Whitney on Language.* Ed. Michael Silverstein. Cambridge, Mass.: MIT Press.

Willey, G., and P. Phillips. 1958. *Method and Theory in American Archaeology.* Chicago: University of Chicago Press.

Wilmsen, E. N. 1989. *Land Filled with Flies: A Political Economy of the Kalahari.* Chicago: University of Chicago Press.

Wilson, Edward Osborne. 1975. *Sociobiology: The New Synthesis.* Cambridge, Mass.: Belknap Press. [2nd ed. 2000.]

——. 1978. *On Human Nature.* Cambridge, Mass.: Harvard University Press.

——. 1996. *Consilience: The Unity of Knowledge.* New York: Knopf.

——. 2000. *Sociobiology: The New Synthesis. 25th Anniversary Edition.* Cambridge, Mass. Belknap Press of Harvard University Press.

——. 2001. "How to Unify Knowledge," In *Unity of Knowledge: The Convergence of Natural and Human Science.* Ed. Antonio R. Damisio, et al. New York: New York Academy of Sciences.

Wolf, Eric. 1981. *Europe and the People without History.* Berkeley: University of California Press.

Wolf, Eric. 1994. "Demonization of anthropologists in the Amazon." *Anthropology Newsletter* (March): 2.

Wolpoff, Milford. 1980. *Paleoanthropology.* New York: Knopf.

Yanagisako, Sylvia J. 1998. "Department of Cultural and Social Anthropology: Vision Statement." *Anthropology Newsletter*, October, 21–22.

Yarrow, T. 2003. "Artefactual Persons: The Relational Capacities of Persons and Things in the Practice of Excavation." *Norwegian Archaeological Review* 36: 65–73.

Zalewski, D. 2000. "Anthropology Enters the Age of Cannibalism." *New York Times*, October 8, Week in Review section.

CONTRIBUTORS

James Clifford is a professor of History of Consciousness at the University of California, Santa Cruz.

Ian Hodder is a professor of Cultural and Social Anthropology at Stanford University.

Rena Lederman is an associate professor of Anthropology at Princeton University.

Daniel A. Segal is the Jean M. Pitzer Professor of Anthropology and a professor of Historical Studies at Pitzer College.

Michael Silverstein is the Charles F. Grey Distinguished Service Professor of Anthropology, Linguistics, and Psychology at the University of Chicago.

Sylvia Yanagisako is a professor of Cultural and Social Anthropology at Stanford University.

INDEX

Adams, William, 81–82, 89

Aesthetic judgment, 69

African Americans, 76 n.17. *See also* Du Bois, W. E. B.

African roots theory. *See* Herskovitz, Melville

Aggression, 56–57, 62

Agnosticism, 24, 25, 39

Altruism, 105

American Anthropological Association, 1, 7, 18, 20 n.2, 21 nn.5, 7, 22 n.14, 33, 45, 79, 86–87, 89, 124 n.18; centenary of, 2; Centennial Commission, 20–21 n.5; departure of biological anthropologists from, 22 n.14; founding of, 98 n.10 (*see also* Boas, Franz); meetings of, 2; presidents of, 2, 95; reorganization of, 3; Tierney/Chagnon controversy and, 56. *See also* Commission to Review the Organizational Structure of the AAA

American Anthropologist, 7, 11, 19 n.2, 22 n.16, 26, 75 n.13, 89, 94–95, 98 n.11

American Council of Learned Societies, 59

American culture: and ancient Greece, 83–84; 91–92; anthropology and, 56, 105; fraternities and, 83–84; immigration and, 60; literature and, 83; Native Americans and, 85, 89–91 (*see also* Native Americans); postcoloniality and, 97 n.6; transnationalism and, 97 n.6. *See also* California; Civil Rights Movement; Knowledge; Vietnam War

American democracy, 84–85

American Ethnological Society, 7, 86

American Ethnologist, 7, 20 n.5, 25

American Historical Association, 33, 45

American Indians. *See* Native Americans

Americanist tradition in anthropology. *See* Anthropology: American

American literature. *See* American culture

American Museum of Natural History. *See* Museums

American nationalism. *See* Nationalism: American

American Revolution, 83, 84

Androcentrism, 96

Animal communication, 63

Anthropological linguistics. *See* Anthropology

Anthropology: American, 16, 32, 36, 38, 44, 46, 78–79, 85, 89–93, 103, 113, 120 n.4, 124 n.18, 129, 133–134; and archaeology (*see* Archaeology); and area studies, 51, 75 n.9; and art history, 47; "Balkanization" of, 78, 97 n.1. (*see also* Science: wars); biocultural, 2, 4, 7, 19 n.1, 20 n.3, 29, 37, 50, 54, 55, 57, 60, 66, 76 n.18, 87, 92, 94, 98 n.13; biological, (*see* Anthropology: biocultural); Boasian, 2, 15, 60, 61, 64, 86, 92; British, 38, 46, 78, 82, 85, 90, 97 n.4, 124 n.19; Central European, 46; and classics, 47; cognitive, 47, 108, 110; and colonialism, 83; as a comparative science, 24, 41, 51, 52, 54, 74 n.4, 93; and consumer research, 70; as "cultural critique," 53; and cultural

Anthropology Society of Washington, 98 n.11

Appadurai, Arjun, 119, 124 n.22, 134

Arabic language. *See* Language

Archaeology, 2, 9; American, 127–130; anthropology and, 18, 29, 44, 46, 47, 54, 62, 64, 75 n.10, 79, 81, 82, 87, 88, 94, 126–140; and art history, 139; behavioral, 127, 128, 129, 136, 139; British, 81, 126; at Cambridge University, 126; and classics, 18, 126, 139; colonialism and, 127; contract, 131; departments of, 126, 135; dialectical approach to, 131; and environmental science, 18; European, 81; feminism and, 131, 133; fieldwork in, 133; and French linguistics and philosophy, 133; and globalization, 132, 140; and heritage, 132–133; historical, 129, 135; and history, 18, 37, 77 n.22, 81, 126, 127, 132, 138; and human biology, 18, 130, 139; and the humanities, 126, 138; and hunter-gatherers (*see* Hunter-gatherers); interpretative, 132; and local communities, 137; and material culture, 132, 135, 136, 138; and metallurgy, 136; as a metaphor in the social sciences, 134–135; museums, 126, 127; nationalism and, 127; Native Americans and, 93, 127, 133; new, 127–128; and new media, 133; and nomadism, 136; and Oriental studies, 126; phenomenological approach to, 131, 132, 139; and philosophy, 138; postprocessual 12, 18, 80, 115, 131–134 (*see also* Hodder, Ian); processual, 128, 129, 130; and psychology, 139; and power, 132; and science, 75 n.10; 130, 138; selectionist, 127, 128, 139; and social variation, 136; and sociology, 133, 138; and technology studies, 138 (*see also* Technology

studies, History); training in, 126, 140. *See also* Chatalhöyük

Archival research. *See* History

Articulation. *See* Disciplinarity

Authenticity, 133

Bachofen, Johann J., 97 n.7

Bacon, Francis, 119 n.1

Baconian tradition. *See* Bacon, Francis

Baker, Lee, 61, 65, 76 n.17

Barbarism, 84, 85

Barnes, R. H., 74 n.4

Barth, Fredrik, 26, 33

Barthes, Roland, 42

Bartu, Ayfer, 138

Benedict, Ruth, 121 n.5

Ben-zvi, Yael, 97 n.6

Biocultural integration. *See* Biocultural synthesis

Biocultural synthesis, 5, 11, 13. *See also* Anthropology: biocultural; Holism; Science

Biology, 11, 12, 25, 28, 31, 45, 53, 68, 69, 77 n.25. *See also* Genetics; Science; Sociobiology

Bloomfield, Leonard, 122 n.12

Boas, Franz, 3, 12, 13, 54, 91, 93, 98 n.12; and Baffin Island fieldwork, 60; and (cosmographic) historicism, 101, 102, 103, 106, 120 n.3, 121 nn.5, 8, 124 n.19; and definition of anthropology, 37; and Durkheim, 121–122 n.9 and discipline boundaries, 29, 59; and Du Bois, 23 n.20, 60, 76 n.17; and establishment of the AAA, 86–87; and historical particularism, 52, 90; and the Humboldtian tradition, 98 n.9; and Kroeber, 121 n.8; and obsolescent languages, 125 n.23; and physical anthropology, 60–61, 65, 74 n.8; and race, 76 n.17. *See also* Anthropology: Boasian

Bohr, Nils, 107

Galison, Peter, 27, 132

Geertz, Clifford, 12, 43, 52–53, 74 n.8, 103, 110, 124 n.20, 132

Gender, 11; hierarchies of, 13; studies of, 25, 53, 64, 93, 96

Genetics: human, 69; molecular, 66, 68, 77 n.25, 104

Geography, 47; department at Harvard University, 34; department at the University of Illinois-Chicago, 67; dialect (*see* Linguistics); political, 35, 36, 136. *See also* Anthropology: and cultural geography

Giddens, Anthony, 132

Gift, 41

Globalization, 24, 35, 41, 42, 57, 124–125 n.22, 128. *See also* Archaeology

Godzich, Wlad, 44

Goodenough, Ward H., 123–124 n.17

Gould, Stephen, 75 n. 11

Governmentality, 28, 42

Graff, Gerald, 31

Gramsci, Antonio, 27, 28; anthropology and, 92

Greenberg, Joseph, 123 n.16

Green movement, 115

Gross, Paul, 68

Habitat selection, 69

Habitus, 25, 31

Haile, Bernard, 91

Hall, Stuart, 28, 36

Handler, Richard, 26

Harris, Marvin, 54, 89, 121 n.8

Harvard University. *See* Geography

Hegemony, 27, 36

Heidegger, Martin, 132

Herder, Johann G. von, 113, 117

Hermeneutical approach in anthropology. *See* Constructivism

Herskovitz, Melville, 76 n.17

Higham, John, 33

Historical particularism. *See* Boas, Franz

Historicism: new, 31, 34, 112

Historiography, 62, 64

History, 10, 11, 25, 35, 112; American 32–33; and anthropology (*see* Anthropology); and archival research, 31; and cliometrics, 33; and "crisis of representation," 33; cultural, 100; departments of, 13, 34, 62; disciplinarian, 119–120 n.1; European vs. American, 8–9, 33; and feminism, 33; and hunter-gatherers (*see* Hunter-gatherers); intellectual, 62; and material culture, 33, 64; and media flows, 33; metahistory, 24; oral, 33; social, 25, 66; and structure, 37, 102; of technology, 135 (*see also* Technology studies); urban, 33; Western, 36; and world system, 33

Hocart, A. M., 124 n.19

Hodder, Ian, 18, 46, 64, 75 n.10, 81

Holism, 9, 10, 11, 13, 16, 19 n.1, 21 n.10, 59, 60, 64, 72–73, 75–76 n.15, 79, 81, 89, 94, 105; strategic, 5 (*see also* Anthropology: four-field; Positivism)

Holy, Ladislau, 74 n.6

Homo sapiens, 12, 104

"Human nature," 14, 15, 57

Human Relations Area Files (HRAF), 52, 54, 121 n.6

Hunter-gatherers, 136

Hybridity, 11, 22 n.18

Iconism, 124 n.20

Identity: studies of, 27, 133. *See also* Nationalism

Incest avoidance, 69, 102, 107–108

Indexicality, 106

Indianology. *See* Native Americans

Indigenous scholarship, 41

Interdisciplinarity. *See* Disciplinarity

Internal Revenue Service, 22 n.14, 89

Internet. *See* Media

Nomadism. *See* Archaeology
Novick, Peter, 31, 32–34

Objectivism. *See* Positivism
Ong, Walter J., 36
Orality, 36. *See also* Literature
Organicism, 39
Ortner, Sherry, 43, 114, 134

Parsons, Talcott, 103
Participant observation. *See* Anthropology: fieldwork
Past: importance of, for geopolitics, 136. *See also* Archaeology
Peabody Museum. *See* Museums
Peasant studies, 9
Persian language. *See* Language
Person: as object of anthropological study, 41
Perspectivalism: antifoundational, 112
Philology. *See* Linguistics
Philosophy, 53, 62, 112; departments of, 34; French, 133; of science, 23 n.21. *See also* Ethics
Phonology, 108–110, 122 n.13; and communication engineering, 122–123 n. 15. *See also* Kinship; Linguistics
Physics, 11, 34, 63; high-energy, 49; particle, 68, 107; social organization of, 96, 132
Piaget, Jean, 62, 120 n.2
Pike, Kenneth, 122 n.14
Pinker, Steven, 57
Political economy, 35, 62
Political science. *See* Science
Positivism, 7, 11, 12, 55; in linguistics, 30. *See also* Anthropology: four-field; Holism; Constructivism
Postcolonialism. *See* Colonialism
Postmodernism, 12, 57, 58, 104, 129
Post-structuralism, 30, 64, 95
Practice theories, 135

Prague school. *See* Jakobson, Roman; Linguistics; Troubetzkoy, Nikolai S.
Praxiology, 113
"Primitive" societies, 14, 37, 38, 40, 44. *See also* Exoticism; Time: and "primitive" peoples; West: and "peoples without history"
Primitivism, 97 n.3
Primates, 8, 11, 63, 105
Psychoanalysis. *See* Anthropology: psychoanalytic
Psychology, 53, 62, 74 n.8, 122 n.9, 123 n.15. *See also* Anthropology: and psychology
Punctuated equilibrium: theory of, 75 n. 11

Rabinow, Paul, 57, 65
Race, 29, 38; as defining issue of anthropology, 60; biological theories of, 12, 60–61, 93; Boas's critique and, 61; cultural theories of, 12, 93, 98 n.13; Darwinism and, 76 n.16, 100; identity and, 9; IQ differences and, 62, 74 n.8; popular ideology of, 61, 92–93; special issue of *American Anthropologist* on, 89; studies of, 25, 61, 64; U.S. court cases and, 61, 76 n.17. *See also* Culture
Racial character, 13
Racism: and antiracism in anthropology, 61, 89, 92; and public policy in the early twentieth century, 60; scientific, 13, 22 n.20, 62; study of, 53
Radcliffe-Brown, Alfred R.: American anthropology and, 91–92; as a functionalist, 96, 102, 120 n.4; "natural science of society" and, 45;
Rational choice theory, 15
Recapitulation, 120 n.3
Reductionism: of the cultural and social to the biological, 11, 68; as scientific method, 68; strong vs. qualified, 63, 69. *See also* Positivism

Reflexive turn in the social sciences. *See* Constructivism

Reflexivity, 41, 112, 133

Relationality, 25

Relativism. *See* Anthropology: Boasian; Durkheim, Émile

Ricouer, Paul, 124 n.20

Romance languages. *See* Language

Rosaldo, Renato, 52–53

"Sacred bundle," 1, 2, 16, 50, 58, 61, 73, 86, 91

Sahlins, Marshall, 42, 43, 75 n.8, 122 n.11, 124 n.22, 127, 132, 136

Sapir, Edward, 12, 29, 91–92

Saussure, Ferdinand de, 30, 39, 101, 109, 110, 122 n.13

Savagery: as an evolutionary stage, 85

"Savage slot," 9, 38, 56, 58, 70

Scheper-Hughes, Nancy, 57, 71

Schiffer, Michael, 129, 131

Schneider, David M., 7, 54, 96, 103, 123 n.16, 124 n.20

Schuchardt, Hugo, 125 n.25

Science: and archaeology (*see* Archaeology); botanical, 100; cognitive, 28, 31, 42, 57, 66, 70, 96; decolonization of, 47; as discursive figure, 55; and humanities, 18, 27, 32, 37, 68, 73, 88, 94, 104, 121 n.8 (*see also* Anthropology); natural, 30, 31; neuroscience, 68, 69; "normal," 13, 15; political, 67; professionalization of, 35; "queer," 13, 23 n.22; social, 18, 27; unity of, 63–64, 68; wars, 27, 51, 65, 68, 112, 124 n.18; zoological, 100

Scientific method, 13, 23 n.21. *See also* Positivism

Searle, John, 70

Segal, Daniel, 19 n.2, 22 n.12, 23 n.22, 50, 72, 73

Seizer, Susan, 23 n.22

Semiology. *See* Anthropology; Language

Semiotics. *See* Anthropology; Linguistics

Service, Elman, 127

Shankland, David, 138

Sibling group, 102

Silverstein, Michael, 16–18, 29, 39, 64, 75 n.10

Smithsonian Institution. *See* Museums

Snow, C. P., 51, 74 n.5

Social structure, 38

Society for Cultural Anthropology, 19 n.2

Sociobiology, 10, 15, 31, 56–58, 67–68, 69, 75 n.8, 104, 105, 120 n.2, 122 n.11

Sociocultural Anthropology Mission Statement. *See* Anthropology department: at New York University

Sociolinguistics: and race discourse (*see* Race); and the Weinreich-Labov tradition, 106

Sociology, 9, 25, 38; functionalist (*see* Parsons, Talcott); of knowledge, 115, 119 n.1. *See also* Anthropology: and sociology

Solidarity: mechanical vs. organic. *See* Durkheim, Émile

Spencer, Herbert, 102

Stanford Humanities Center: "Have the Disciplines Collapsed?" conference, 31

Steward, Julian H., 106, 121 n.8

Stocking, George W., Jr., 2–3, 16–17, 21 n.6, 29, 39, 59–60, 86–87

Strathern, Marilyn, 32, 75 n.8

Structuralism. *See* Anthropology; Linguistics; Post-Structuralism

Structure: and history. *See* History

Students: doctoral, 6; and professors, 22 n.13; teaching assistants, 6; undergraduate, 6

Subaltern studies, 35, 112

Subcultures: studies of, 44

Library of Congress Cataloging-in-Publication Data
Unwrapping the sacred bundle : reflections on the disciplining of
anthropology / edited by Daniel A. Segal and Sylvia J. Yanagisako.
p. cm.
Includes bibliographical references and index.
ISBN 0-8223-3462-3 (cloth : alk. paper)
ISBN 0-8223-3474-7 (pbk. : alk. paper)
1. Anthropologists—Training of. 2. Anthropologists—Education.
3. Physical anthropology. 4. Ethnoarchaeology. 5. Ethnology.
6. Anthropological linguistics. I. Segal, Daniel Alan, 1958–.
II. Yanagisako, Sylvia Junko, 1945–.
GN41.8.U58 2005
301–dc22
2004025081